A History of Scotland

Wi

Book Three

Oxford University Press 1985

Oxford University Press, Walton Street, Oxford OX2 6DP

London   New York   Toronto
Delhi   Bombay   Calcutta   Madras   Karachi
Nairobi   Dar es Salaam   Cape Town
Kuala Lumpur   Singapore   Hong Kong   Tokyo
Melbourne   Auckland

and associated companies in
Beirut   Berlin   Ibadan   Mexico City   Nicosia

Oxford is a trademark of Oxford University Press
© William Moffat 1985

First published 1985
ISBN 0 19 917044 4

Typeset by Tradespools Limited, Frome, Somerset.
Printed in Hong Kong

Contents

James I – James III

The King's return

James I, thirty years old, had been King of Scotland for eighteen years. His whole reign had been spent in English captivity, not as a common prisoner, of course, more as a guest, royally entertained. He was tutored in the princely sports and pastimes, in foreign languages and the arts of music, speech and writing. His keen interest in military engineering was balanced by his skill on the harp and in composing poetry. He crossed the border and entered his kingdom in the April of 1424. With Joan, his Queen and an escort of nobles they reached Melrose by the fifth of that month. Those of his people who lined the way were soon to learn that this was a different kind of ruler from any they had known.

The two Roberts had been older men and the Regent Albany, James's ambitious uncle, older still. Here was a strong king, young and vigorous, a man determined to be master of his realm. But with mounting anger and disgust he learned that in Scotland there was no law save that of brute force. His kingdom was 'a den of thieves' and crime, however bad, went unpunished. 'Justice, as if outlawed, lay in exile outwith the bounds of the realm'.

Crime

And there was worse to come. It became clear to James that crimes went unpunished and justice was absent because the very people, nobles and others in high places, whose duty it was to keep the King's Peace were the chief offenders. The population was preyed upon by those who should protect it. In anger, he exclaimed, 'If God grant me life and aid, be it the life of a dog, there shall be no place in all my realm where the key shall not keep the castle and the bracken-bush the cow!'

Albany's regency

For fourteen of the years that James spent in exile Scotland had been governed by his uncle, the Duke of Albany, the man who had been such a threat to the young Prince's safety. Though only a regent, he had lived and ruled as a king, hoping one day to be just that. He was, after all, the next in line to the throne and because of these royal hopes he had done little to get James released. Yet, for all his faults, Albany had kept reasonable order in the land, being firm where he

A typical harp of the period

Portrait of James I

dared and cunning where necessary. The barons were at peace, and the common folk liked him because he did not collect taxes! In the uneasy quiet of his rule there was time again for good harvests and prospering business. Scotland's first university was founded at St Andrews early in 1412. For the most part, Scottish swords were drawn only outside the kingdom. They helped the French defeat the English at the Battle of Bauge, and had other successes and other failures.

Trouble in the Highlands

But there *was* trouble at home too, not in the borders this time but beyond the Highland line. One of Albany's nephew's, Donald, Lord of the Isles, had a claim to the Earldom of Ross in the North, which conflicted with the Regent's own claim. Donald decided to settle the dispute in the usual way – by force. He gathered an army and in the summer of 1411 marched through the Great Glen to Inverness and the Earldom. Welcomed in Ross, and having seized Inverness he moved south-east across the Spey and through the lands of Mar. At Harlaw on the north bank of the River Ury not twenty miles from Aberdeen, which he intended to plunder, Donald was faced by the Earl of Mar, son of the Lord of Badenoch and just as much the wolf. On the 24th July, the highlanders of Clan Donald armed with bows and axes, swords and dirks, hurled themselves against the knights and spearmen of Mar. All that afternoon and into the late dusk of a summer evening the riot of thrusting lance and slashing sword filled the warm air. Neither side would give way. When at last darkness fell and they both withdrew from the red soaked patch of moorland, each thought the other had won. The slaughter is remembered as Red Harlaw and it settled nothing. Both Regent Albany and Donald, Lord of the Isles continued to claim the Earldom of Ross, Albany for his son and Donald for himself.

5

A new regent

But it was in 1420 that the real troubles came to Scotland. The Duke of Albany, by then a vigorous old man of eighty-three, died leaving his son Murdoch to succeed to his title and to the regency. It was a disaster. The new Duke of Albany was quite unable to rule the kingdom. The day of the robber barons returned. Free to raid at will, they plundered and terrorised burgh and countryside alike. They seized for themselves all but a tiny part of the crown revenues. Unrest and anger spread through the nation like a plague. Lairds and free men were near to open revolt when at last their king came home.

First moves

James acted at once. Even before his coronation, at Scone on 21st May 1424, he had one of Murdoch's sons under lock and key. A few days afterwards he had called his first parliament at Perth. There he passed laws against those who would conduct private wars, enlist private armies, rebel, refuse to aid the King against rebels, or make unlawful demands on others.

He also created officers of the law who would enforce it and be punished if they failed in their duty.

Within a year of his coronation James arrested Albany and his two sons on real or not so real charges of treason and executed them. The proud clan chiefs he treated in much the same way. More than forty of them were summoned to a special parliament at Inverness. One by one they came, each with his train of followers as befitted a Highland lord. Clan Donald was there and Campbell and Mackay – almost all the tribes of the north. One by one, these proud leaders were hurled into the dungeon-pit. Three of them were hanged. The rest were freed after a short but memorable stay in prison. All but one learned the lesson and made their peace. Alexander of the Isles, son of Donald, out for revenge, turned loose the men of Clan Donald to burn and plunder Inverness. The King marched against him at once and in the marshes of Lochaber completely defeated him. Two months later before the high altar of Holyrood Abbey, Alexander went on his knees before his King to offer a naked sword, that he might be struck down where he knelt. His surrender was accepted and the Lord of the Isles went to prison in Tantallon Castle at North Berwick. He was later restored to his lands and title and managed to remain in the King's favour.

The Inverness Parliament

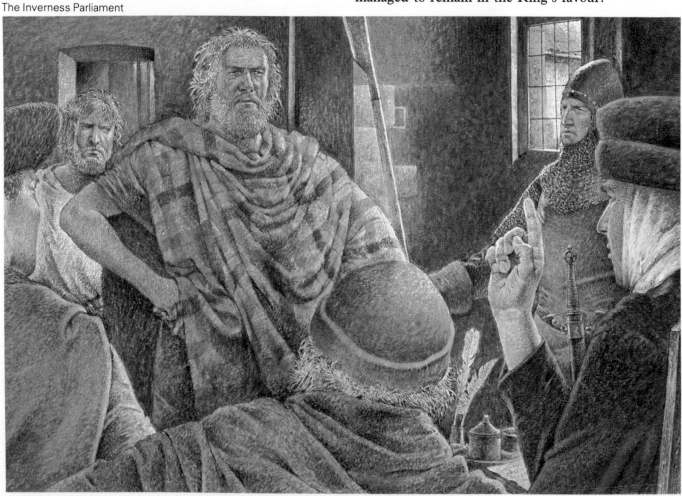

The rule of law

James made it very clear to everyone that all his subjects, from the most humble to the highest, were subject to law. And he had done more. Justice was now available to all, poor and rich alike. Those who could not afford a lawyer to defend them had one provided free. The King expanded parliament and improved government. New laws were kept under observation and changed when necessary. All this he did in four short years, more than most of Scotland's kings managed in a lifetime. But he made more enemies too.

Coat of arms of Sir Robert Graham

Sir Robert Graham

Thirteen years after his return to Scotland, James and his Queen spent Christmas at Blackfriars Monastery in Perth. As the royal couple prepared to retire for the night on 20th February 1437, eight shadowy forms were moving quietly outside the monastery walls. In the misty darkness of that winter night planks were slid noiselessly over the moat to form a bridge. Sir Robert Graham, whom James had imprisoned when Albany and his sons were arrested was looking for revenge. The hate Sir Robert bore the King fed on the wrongs done to his nephew when James had unfairly seized his lands. The first warning the King had was the heavy clank of mailed men approaching swiftly. James had no weapons and the bolts for the door had been removed. He snatched a poker from the hearth and frantically levered up some loose floor boards. With some difficulty he squeezed through the narrow gap and into the drain which ran beneath the chamber.

Escape would have been his had not the outlet been sealed to prevent the loss of more of the King's tennis balls. As it was he could only hide there and wait. The Queen and her ladies did what they could to resist the intruders. Catherine Douglas is said to have thrust her arm through iron straps that should have held the bolt. She must have suffered cruelly when the door was burst in. The King's hiding place was soon discovered and he was dragged out and butchered by Sir Robert and his henchmen.

Queen Joan was wounded defending her husband, but she survived and set out to bring the brutal murderers to justice. James's 'milk and white dove', his 'freshest and fairest of flowers' became a demon in her vengeance and, within a month all were taken. Three days of merciless torture were borne by the assassins before they were allowed to die.

In the madness of his hatred, Graham had thought that the people would rejoice at the death of a tyrant King. He believed it to the very end. But to the people, James was no tyrant. He was their deliverer. For he had brought law and order, security and protection to a country which had become a 'den of thieves.' It was at the execution of Graham and his cutthroats that the people rejoiced, chanting –

Sir Robert Graham
Slew our King
God give him shame.

A sixteenth century fresco showing the court of James I

King James II

Now to the throne came James II, to be crowned and anointed, not at Scone but in Holyrood Abbey, on 25th March 1437. But this James was only six and would not rule for many years yet. Once more the government would rest in the hands of a regent. This time it was to be Archibald the Earl of Douglas, Duke of Touraine and Count of Longueville, Lord of Galloway and Annandale, The Lieutenant General of Scotland, to give him his full style. He was perhaps the richest and most powerful noble in the whole realm. He was appointed by the High Council to continue the dead King's strong government. And he was aided by the Chancellor, Bishop Cameron. They were both answerable to Queen Joan who naturally also had the care of her child, the infant King James II. But it did not work. The regent was a Douglas and could not see why he should labour hard to keep the kingdom for a Stewart. He was a bad choice, and Scotland slumped into a time of misery once more. Lawlessness, plague and famine racked the nation and as always the common folk suffered most. Earls and barons fought out of greed, and what little the regent may have done to stop the conflict ended when he fell victim to the plague in 1439.

Almost at once there began a savage power struggle between two lesser nobles. They were the keepers of the great castles of Edinburgh and Stirling. First, one kidnapped eight year old James from the other who had been his proper guardian. Then, both got together in their greed and murdered the new Earl of Douglas who seemed a threat to their ambitions. He was just sixteen. And so the long brawl continued, to the nation's cost, and was only interrupted by the invasion of an English army. Dunbar and Dumfries were burnt and plundered. With Englishmen to fight, the nobles set aside their own strife. Within the month they had destroyed Alnwick and Warkworth in Northumberland.

The young Earl of Douglas and his only brother David, foolishly accepted an invitation to dinner at Edinburgh Castle with the two nobles and the young King. It was a fine meal but for 'afters' there was a fake trial and a real execution. The Douglas boys lost their heads for invented treason. The young James watched in horror, but learned a grim lesson. The treacherous affair came to be known as the Black Dinner.

The King takes control

The kingdom was still ablaze with private war in 1449 when at last the eighteen year old James II stepped forward and took a wife, Mary of Gueldres, and the firm control of his realm's government. He was called Fiery Face for the red birthmark that covered one cheek. He was fiery at heart too. As his father had done before him he smashed the power of the nobles by every means open to him, including the blatant murder of a guest at the supper table.

James had learned well, though at his own 'Black Supper' there was no fake trial and no formal execution. That night at Stirling Castle, William, Earl of Douglas, the most powerful noble in the land was commanded to cut his bond with the rebels. He refused bluntly, even defiantly. In a fit of rage, made worse by the wine, James screamed 'Since you will not, I will!' He hurled himself on Douglas and buried his royal dagger in the proud Earl's neck. The blood flowed far beyond that room when William's brother burnt and plundered Stirling town in revenge for the King's wild treachery, though the common townsfolk had, of course, played no part in it.

Peace

By 1455, James II had brought his kingdom to order and was able to govern in peace. Common folk could again go about their living under the protection of the King's Law. They enjoyed more security now, for lands held by rent remained with the tenant for the agreed time even when sold to another landowner. Though all able bodied men between sixteen and sixty had to be ready to defend the border, those too poor to be properly armed were not required to cross it.

And James tried to encourage archery by fining those who missed practices and using the fines to buy refreshment for those who attended. Even this could not take the Scots from their national pastimes – football and golf. At Glasgow in 1451 Scotland's second university was founded and James granted it a charter two years later.

A History of Scotland

England

In the south the dark clouds were gathering once again. There was talk, loud and proud, of English Lordship over Scotland, and a letter was received by the Scottish King addressing him as 'James, calling himself King of Scotland . . . !' He was even called 'a rebel'. James, was enraged. He rode south, twenty miles into Northumberland, destroying seventeen strongholds before returning. He had made his point and a truce was hastily agreed by the English King, who removed the noble responsible for the foolish letter.

In 1460 James decided to take back Roxburgh Castle, England's only foothold in Scotland. On Sunday, 3rd August, the great host of Scotland was arrayed in full battle order outside the castle's mighty walls. James's great guns were trained on their target and ready. To celebrate the arrival of the Queen, the guns were ordered to fire a royal salute. James in curiosity stood close by a cannon called 'the Lion'. It blew up and the King was killed instantly by its exploding fragments.

An old prophecy had foretold the fall of Roxburgh Castle to a dead man. It came true that August when Scotland's army honoured their King by carrying on the siege in his name. On the 8th day of the month the castle was taken and pulled down stone by stone. The English had been driven from Teviotdale and the Scots rejoiced.

On the 10th August 1460, James III was crowned in Kelso Abbey, hardly a stone's throw from where his father had died. But he was only eight.

Early years

For several years the wise and statesmanlike Bishop Kennedy, with Queen Mary, the young King's mother, kept the Kingdom in peace. By 1465 both Queen and Bishop had died and the following year King James III, now fourteen, was seized by some of the lesser nobles, led by the Boyds of Kilmarnock. At Edinburgh in October 1466 Lord Boyd, who had been the tutor to the King on military matters, became the King's Guardian and Keeper of the Royal Castles. All power now lay with him but he did not abuse it. He even managed to arrange for young James III to marry Margaret of Denmark, getting Orkney and Shetland in place of a promised dowry.

With his new Queen, James III now took in hand the affairs of state and began, as those before him had done, to bend the realm to his will. But this James had not really the character or strength for such business. He was not a soldier, not even a horseman. He was bored by jousting and hunting, shooting arrows and fencing, and was genuinely disgusted by warfare. But he was intelligent and started well enough. He confirmed Orkney and Shetland as part of his realm, though at first they were given only until Margaret's unpaid dowry of 60,000 florins was settled. Scotland was now bigger than it had ever been or would be for it included not only these northernmost Isles, but also for the moment Berwick, which had been returned by the English. And he made a treaty with Edward IV of England which put an end to the treason planned by the exiled Earl of Douglas and his ally in the north, John, Lord of the Isles.

Guns During these peaceful years, James II had more time for his great interest in the not very peaceful subject of guns. These new weapons had served him well, finally bringing the barons to order. Their strongholds could not withstand the pounding delivered by such guns as 'Mons Meg' which still stands by Edinburgh Castle. With a deafening thunderclap of smoke and flame this huge cannon could fire an enormous stone or iron ball up to two miles, striking terror into the hearts of the stoutest garrison. The great castles of Threave and Abercorn fell before such assaults and the over-mighty Douglas tribe was at last brought down.

10

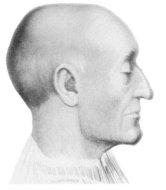

above: Drawing of Bishop Kennedy
right: Portrait of James III

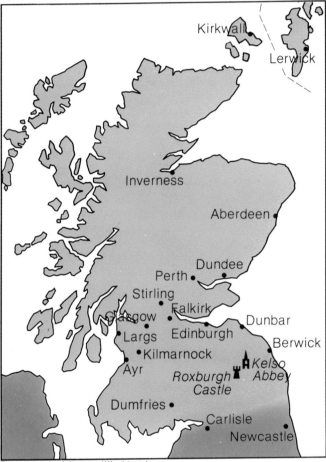

The extent of James III's kingdom

An uneasy reign

But James III was not a successful king, though why he failed is not easy to see. His interests were in fine music and fine buildings and fine clothes, so perhaps he was uneasy with the nobles, who believed that true kingship lay in ceremony and fighting. Perhaps he was too ready to pardon rather than punish, and too suspicious of everyone, even his two brothers. Whatever the reasons, James III soon found himself unable to defeat his nobles or to make them his friends. Even his son turned against him. In the end the matter was settled on the field of battle – or rather, just off it.

Death of James

On 11th June 1488, James brought the rebels to battle, close by the place where Robert Bruce won his glorious victory at Bannockburn. The King, a most unwilling warrior, faced his rebellious son. The armies closed, James's loyal highlanders and his men from the burghs against the steady spears and lances of the border men – north against south, father against son.

Where the little Sauchie Burn twists its way through the plain below Stirling Castle, in a frenzy of hacking and stabbing the great mass of men swayed back and forward. The King's men began to lose ground, a pace or two, and then a pace or two more. By nightfall they had withdrawn into the darkness of Tor Wood.

In the confusion of retreat James fled the field alone, or perhaps his horse simply bolted. The result was the same, for after a short frantic gallop he was thrown from his saddle. Stunned, James was carried by a local miller and his wife to their cottage nearby where he asked for a priest. He was brought a man who *said* he was a priest. But James received no comfort from this man, only a stab through the heart. His son, fleeing before a counter-attack by the King's forces, was suddenly James IV of Scotland.

James III is carried to his deathbed

Worksection

James I – James III
Understand Your Work

The King's return
1 What age was James I when he first became King?
2 Where did he spend the first eighteen years of his reign?
3 How was he treated in captivity?
4 What were his interests?
5 When did King James return to Scotland?
6 Where was he on the 5th April, 1424?
7 What did the common folk think of this new arrival?
8 What did James think of what was happening in his kingdom?
9 What did James discover to be the main reason for the break down in law and order?
10 What did he vow to do about it?

Albany's regency and after
1 For how long did the Duke of Albany rule Scotland as regent?
2 What was his secret ambition?
3 How did this affect the release of James from English captivity?
4 What sort of ruler was the Duke of Albany?
5 Why did the common folk like him?
6 What happened at St. Andrews during his rule?
7 Where did the Scots take part in fighting, and who were they helping?
8 What was remembered as Red Harlaw?
9 Who succeeded to the regency after the Duke of Albany died?
10 What happened under the new regent?

First moves and the Rule of Law
1 What was James' earliest move against the law breakers?
2 Where was James' first parliament held?
3 What laws did he frame in that parliament?
4 How did he make sure his laws were kept?
5 How did James deal with the powerful highland clan chiefs?
6 Did this make all the clan chiefs obey him?
7 How did Alexander of the Isles show his resistance to the King?
8 How did King James deal with him?
9 How did the King make it possible for poor people to find justice under his rule of law?
10 How long did the King take to develop his rule of law?

Sir Robert Graham
1 When did the King meet his death?
2 Where did this happen?
3 How did James attempt to escape?
4 What part did Catherine Douglas play in the affair?
5 What happened to the assassins?
6 What did the common people think of Sir Robert Graham?
7 Why had James I been popular with the people?

King James II
1 How old was James II when he was crowned in Holyrood Abbey?
2 Who ruled the kingdom while James was too young?
3 Was he a good choice?
4 What happened in 1493?
5 In what condition was Scotland at this time?
6 What interrupted the fighting amongst the Scottish nobles?
7 When did James II finally take control of his kingdom?
8 How did he end the fighting amongst the Scottish nobles?
9 What happened to the Earl of Douglas at Stirling Castle?

Peace and War
1 How long did it take James II to restore law and order to his kingdom?
2 How did this affect the common people?
3 What did the King do to improve conditions for the tenant farmers?
4 What special rule applied to poor folk when it came to military service?
5 How did James try to encourage archery and why did he have to do this?
6 When did he grant a charter to Glasgow University?
7 How did James II answer English claims to lordship over Scotland?
8 Why did James lay siege to Roxburgh Castle?
9 How did the old prophecy come true at this siege?

James III
1 At what age was the third James crowned?
2 By whom was the kingdom ruled while James III was a child?
3 How did James differ from the previous two kings of that name?
4 What were his main interests?
5 Why was he not a more successful King?
6 When and how did his reign end?

Use Your Imagination

1 Why do you think royal persons were well treated even when in captivity?

2 What does 'Key keep the castle and the bracken bush the cow' mean?

3 What kind of cunning tactics do you suppose the Duke of Albany used to keep the nobles at peace under his control?

4 Why did James I outlaw private armies?

5 Why do you think James treated the proud clan chiefs so roughly?

6 James I made more useful laws in four years than most of Scotland's kings managed in a lifetime? Why do you suppose he also made more enemies?

7 Why do you think the sixteen year old Earl of Douglas was murdered at the Black Dinner?

8 How do you know that golf and football must have been very popular in James II's reign?

9 Why do you think a stone castle was a poor defence against cannon? What special danger would defenders suffer when the ball crashed against stonework?

10 What was it about James III that allowed him to start well in his reign and then do badly?

Further Work

1 Discuss in your group what material might be used to construct a good defence against cannon fire. (It has to be readily available to James II's people!) Prepare plans of your cannon-proof castle, to display to the class.

2 Find out why Renfrew is called the 'Cradle of the Stewarts.'

3 When Sir Robert Graham murdered James I the people chanted the rhyme –

> Sir Robert Graham
> Slew our King
> God give him shame.

And they had another rhyme for the Black Dinner when the young Earl of Douglas and his brother were murdered in Edinburgh Castle –

> Edinburgh Castle, Town and Tower
> God grant thou sink for sin,
> And that even for the black dinner
> Earl Douglas got therein.

Try to write your own rhyme for some event in history, perhaps the stabbing of James III (p. 11) or the murder of William, Earl of Douglas at Stirling Castle (p. 9) or the death of James II when the cannon exploded (p. 10) or something you choose.

4 Try to arrange a visit to Edinburgh Castle where you will see Mons Meg, which was forged in Belgium and imported by James II, and many other interesting exhibits too.

A Time of Change

James IV

When the fourth James took the throne at Scone on 26th June 1488, he was almost sixteen. For a short time there was a Guardian and the usual struggle for power began. But James soon made it clear that control of the realm was his, young or not. Instead of bloodshed James chose talk, and by pardon and good sense he brought nobles together around his throne. There was peace.

The land

James's Scotland had seen little change in more than two centuries. There were more burghs now but most people still lived on the land, and worked on the land as their fathers and their fathers before them had done. Wooden ploughs turned long furrows in the tired soil of narrow hillside fields. The valleys were left to marsh and reed while man and beast toiled on the slopes above, where the drainage was better. The land they tilled was rented from the landlord. The landlord would rarely lease the land for periods of more than five years at a time. Then the farmer could be evicted. Some had no leases at all and could be put out at any time. It paid them all to be on good terms with the laird. It was not the kind of arrangement which encouraged families to build good homes and develop their farms. At the day's end they found their comfort in the smokey warmth of low dark hovels of turf and thatch. During miserable winters their homes were shared with the few cattle not slaughtered and salted at Martinmas in November. A hundred acres or so called a ploughgate, was worked by kinfolk or partners who shared the plough and provided the beasts to pull it. Eight oxen were needed or perhaps four with two horses. Their earthen dwellings clustered close to form a little township. The crops they raised were still oats and barley, and now some wheat, peas and beans too, since James I made this compulsory in 1426.

Farming

The huddle of cottages stood handy for the most fertile part of the ploughgate. This was the infield. Further off on the higher rougher slopes where the land was poorer, lay the outfield. How big the rich infield was, compared with the outfield, depended on how fertile the hillside soil was.

Ploughing

The whole ploughgate was divided into small portions so that each would receive equal share of the good earth and the not so good. Every farmer had strips of land from every part of the ploughgate, which was fair but not always convenient. They were long and narrow to suit the plough – in England usually about two hundred and twenty paces (200m) – a furlong, which was about as far as the animals might pull before requiring a break. In Scotland where the ground is hillier and heavier, broken by more rock outcrops and little burns, the strips were shorter.

Because eight oxen were needed to heave the great wooden ploughs through the heavy soil, communities were formed, with members providing one or perhaps two beasts. They came together for the ploughing season and worked each rig in rotation, one from each member's holding, then another and so on. No one member had the advantage of being finished much sooner than another. But there the teamwork ended. When it came to sowing, tending and reaping, it was every man for himself.

It was not the most efficient means of soil cultivation but grain was produced which provided the Scots with their daily bread and their ale. In the very good years they even had produce for export but usually there was barely enough. From their flocks and herds came milk, butter and cheese; fleeces and skins for clothing; bone and horn for tools and ornaments; salted meat and tallow lamps for long dark winters.

There was no real system of cropping for the poorer slopes. Here, a portion of the land was sown year after year until it became exhausted. It was then left fallow until the grazing herds restored its quality whilst another portion was cultivated. The infield was different. There was no rest here for the soil; the crops were changed – perhaps oats for the first two years and then barley. Before sowing the barley, the land was fertilised with farmyard manure. Then it was oats, oats, barley all over again. Different parts of the infield had different crops each season so that all crops were grown every year including the wheat, peas and beans that the law demanded.

The Burghs

And it was a healthier living than was to be found in the burghs. They were bigger now and grander but dirtier than ever – a breeding ground for disease. They were still all of the one pattern though of different sizes, as in David I's time. From the towngate ran the one main market street lined on both sides with tightly packed wooden houses, two storeys tall and divided only by dark alleys and narrow lanes.

Burghs were still very close communities, like clubs. Burgesses were not simply people who lived in towns. They were required to perform duties and services for the privileges they received. Anyone offending against the community could be expelled and have his house torn down.

The whole place lived, worked and played together. They rose with the sun and retired to the skirl of the town piper and the beat of his drummer. They shared croplands and common grazing in the town's acres, cutting the same heather for thatching and peat for burning. There was a burgh mill for grinding corn – the profits went to the common good fund – and sometimes fishing rights on a nearby river.

Trade

Trade was the reason for the burghs' existence and great care was taken to see that all the burgesses had equal opportunities to gain from the town business. Unexpected cargoes were publicly released for sale so that everyone had the same chance to buy, or to sell when a ship was leaving with exports. No private bargains or secret deals were permitted.

Town life

From the upper floors of their houses the burgesses could look out beyond the town walls, on the town acres where their livestock grazed and their crops grew. They were all still farmers. But so many people living in one place could not hope to find support from their burgh muir alone. They depended on the nearby countryside and its farmers who brought their spare produce to sell at the open market, one day per week. Prices were controlled as was the quality of the goods and food they needed. Hoarding was not allowed.

And in the market place other needs were served too. There was a church to pray in, a tolbooth jail to repent in and the market cross where the fate of wrong-doers – disgrace, discomfort, even execution – could be witnessed. Here too, grizzly displays were made: the severed heads and limbs of those who, in the struggle for power, had lost too often or had not repented fast enough, and thus were traitors. But there was also room for celebration, feast days and holy days when the townsfolk and their country neighbours joined in the dancing and singing to the music of the burgh minstrels.

Disease

But most of all there was squalor. Everywhere garbage and filth were piled high. The wider the market street, the bigger the midden it became. Rats and mice infested the rotting heaps and the air hung heavy with the odour of decay. Because the causes of disease were not understood, infection swept through the crowded burghs time after time, plague upon plague, stilling the noise and bustle of the market place. New public health laws restricted movement of people and cattle during epidemics; children were to be kept in and the streets cleared of dogs and swine; market stalls were closed and special cleaners were appointed for infected houses and streets.

Shipping

Despite all its drawbacks town life thrived. Seventy or so of the burghs were seaports and through these Scotland sent out her exports of hides and wool; salmon, herring and other fish; cloth of a coarse texture; salt, coal and even some pearls, to Belgium, France, Italy, Poland, Germany and of course England. And they imported silk, satin and damask, and velvet, gold and silver and iron too, jewellery and wine. And always there were weapons, new and better guns, the powder to charge them, and the trained men to fire them. War and feud were never far away. And it showed. On the high ground across the kingdom stood warning beacons, fuelled and ready, at the touch of a flame, to blaze forth their call to war.

Fishing

These seaports were also Scotland's centres for fishing, and they now also resounded to the noise of the building of ships. Carpenters laboured with saw and hammer, adze and drill in the urgent construction of a fishing fleet, at James IV's command. Ships of twenty tons would net a fine harvest of silver herring from Scotland's coastal water. Wealth would come to the kingdom by the improved sales of fish to other countries. And the King could always find another use for such boats, and the men who sailed them, in time of war.

The landscape

Nor had the landscape changed greatly through these centuries, though trees were fewer now. Large woodland areas had been stripped for ships, halls and fuel. But further off the great forests still held the land. The brooding stone keeps and towers of nobles and lairds were more plentiful. Now walled courtyards had been added, and greater comfort provided inside – still very much the fortress but now more of a house as well. Land and water still offered their wealth – rivers that teemed with fish, and in the hills, moors and forests, where wild game could be hunted. There was peat for fuel and coal too, and turf and stone for building.

Transport and movement were still difficult though the king's highways took carts and carriages between burghs and castles and there were more bridges now. But still the waterways were best for travel and for carrying goods.

Through all Europe great changes were taking place and Scotland, though at the outermost edge, was changing too. A new King had been crowned and he meant to see that his realm would take its proper place in this new world. Of all the Stewarts, James IV was loved the best. He was an exciting King, young and brave, full of energy and interested in all new ideas.

Medicine

He encouraged learning. Scotland's third university was founded at Aberdeen in 1495, one more than in England at that time. It was to provide instruction not only in the arts, religion and law, but also in medicine. It was the first university in Britain to have a medical school. Unfortunately, the type of medicine taught there was more fashionable than useful. The surgeons and barbers of Edinburgh were more practical. When the College of Surgeons was formed there in 1506 they had the sole right to sell a new invented medicine called *whisky* and also a yearly supply of criminals' corpses to dissect and explore, 'since,' as James said, 'every man aucht to know the nature and substance of everything that he workis, or ellis he is negligent.' James IV was ahead of his time.

Portrait of James IV

A sixteenth century woodcut showing surgical instruments

Education

There was an Education Act too, Scotland's first by which the wealthier lairds were required to send their eldest sons, when nine years old, to school until they mastered Latin and understood the Law. It meant of course that there must have been schools for them to attend, perhaps as many as one in each burgh. The idea was to ensure that those who administered justice were properly trained in the Law. Anyone failing to obey the new Act could be fined £20 – nearer to a thousand pounds to-day.

Printing

By 1507, Scotland had its first printing press, set up in the Southgate of Edinburgh by Walter Chepman, a legal clerk, and Andrew Myller, a bookseller. They were granted a patent by the King to print books of Law, and Acts of Parliament, chronicles, and books of prayer. The legal books proved too complicated but among the works that did come from their press were two volumes of the beautiful Aberdeen Breviary. This book informed priests of the special differences there were in performing the Mass on each of the Scottish Saints' Days and Feast Days and provided stories of the saints' lives. Also from this shop in the Southgate came the published poems and ballads of Robert Henryson and William Dunbar, two of Scotland's greatest poets.

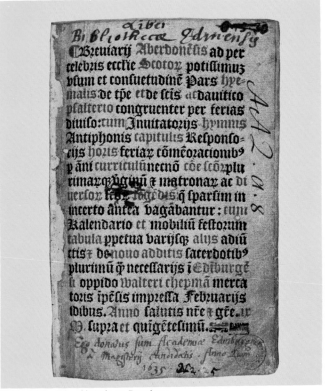

Title page of the Aberdeen Breviary

James's wedding

The early part of James IV reign was a time for poetry and song, for art, music and dance. And never more so than at his wedding to Margaret Tudor, the thirteen year old sister of Henry VIII to be. James enjoyed spending. He would ride to every quarter of his kingdom with his dazzling court, inventors and musicians, scholars and poets, designers and builders. To those in need he gave generously – the lame and blind, those whose crops were damaged by royal horses or those who had been injured in the service of the King. He even rode the 150 miles from Stirling to Elgin alone, to test the strength of his laws.

When it came to his wedding the celebration was spectacular. Princess Margaret left Richmond Palace on 2nd July 1503. She was escorted by her father King Henry VII, and the Royal Court of England, as far as the Manor House of the Countess of Richmond at Collyweston. From there the child-bride began her slow and stately progress to her new home. By the 3rd of August she had reached Dalkeith Castle and was greeted there by the King of Scots, her husband-to-be. She met James again the following day at Newbattle. After refreshment and conversation with Margaret, he left, impressing all who saw him go by leaping astride his horse, spurring forward, and leaving his escort to follow if they could.

The wedding of James IV and Princess Margaret

On the 8th of August the marriage took place in Holyrood Abbey. There before the high altar James received his child queen. The King wore a robe of shining white damask, figured in gold, over a jacket slashed in crimson satin and edged in black velvet. Margaret wore a gown of white and gold, bordered in crimson velvet and a gold crown made specially for her. Her long red hair fell loosely about her shoulders and down past her waist.

William Dunbar wrote a poem in honour of the magnificent occasion called the Thistle and the Rose. He addresses the new Queen, 'Now fair, fairest of every fair', but he was not being strictly honest. Margaret was not 'fairest of the fair' by any means. She was a rather short plump and thoroughly spoiled little madam whose pout betrayed her not very pleasant nature. It was later said of her that she had all the faults of her family, the Tudors, but none of their brains. But James was patient with her, when, for example, she required walls of palaces to be plastered to her liking or even when on one occasion twenty-four carts were required to carry her dresses to Edinburgh from Linlithgow.

James too, was not being strictly honest. The splendour of the wedding which impressed the English, as it was meant to, concealed his shortage of cash. Cloth of gold gowns that cost, in to-day's money, £65,000 could be ill-afforded by a country still suffering from recent wars. But it was money spent in the spirit of the time, a spirit which would drive Scotland forward.

Building projects

It was a time of building too. James had a new palace constructed at Holyrood. And at Stirling, Falkland and Linlithgow splendid new buildings were added to the royal properties. Castles too were rebuilt, at least in part, at Craigmillar in Edinburgh, Caerlaverock on the Solway Firth and Crichton, Huntly and many more.

Ships

And the building was not only on land. A new navy was planned by James which would police the Scottish trade routes and fishing grounds, and put down piracy. It could also be used to commit acts of piracy! In 1505, the King built naval dockyards at the Pool of Airth, about eight miles east of Stirling, and at Newhaven beside Leith. James's first real man-of-war was the *Margaret*, named after the Queen. It took more than two years to build and was armed with twenty-one guns. But it was nothing compared with what was to come later.

Cutaway illustration of typical warship of the period.

In 1507 great oaks were falling all over Fife, to be stripped and floated across the Forth to Newhaven. Here the shipwrights laid a mightier keel than ever before. Great ribs curved skywards all along its length to which the heavy hull planking was nailed. The rasp of the saw and the bang of the hammer filled the yard, year in, year out, as the largest warship ever to have been built in Scotland slowly took shape. The *Michael* was launched in 1511, seventy-five metres in length and eleven across. She was square rigged with four masts, the main one towering almost eighty metres above the deck. She was armed with at least fifteen heavy cannon and countless lighter guns. It took a crew of three hundred to sail the proud *Michael* and she could carry one thousand armed soldiers. No warship afloat was more powerful. She was tested by James firing a cannon ball at her, which failed even to shake the great ship. With flags, pennants and banners flying from every mast and spar, and the red and gold of the Lion Rampant above them all, the *Michael* was the pride of navy and nation alike.

A model of the 'Great Michael'

Edinburgh

With the King's favoured home in Edinburgh, that city now became Scotland's capital. From there James could look out to north and south over a kingdom more at peace within itself and with England than it had been for many many years; a kingdom of merchants and craftsmen, poets and priests, artists and artisans, scholars, soldiers and surgeons, and of common folk who would please their King with gifts as he rode by. The new learning and new thought, called the Renaissance, that lit the minds of men all over Europe, had spilled some of its brightness on the Scottish court.

Braun and Hogenburg's map of 'Edinburgum, Scotiae Metropolis', 1582, seen from south of the present Royal Infirmary of Edinburgh

A kingdom at peace

Trouble with England

Year by year, since Henry VIII had come to his father's throne in 1509, the peace between England and Scotland had grown more fragile. Border raids and feuds again burned a trail of waste across the countryside. In the spring of 1513, Henry, his heart set on glory, was dreaming of the conquest of France. He was joined by Spain, Germany and others in a Holy League. But there was nothing holy about it. Its members were always ready to betray one another and their purpose was always personal gain.

By the terms of the Auld Alliance, James had to support the French king, and envoys from France were asking for aid by early summer. They brought not only their king's official appeal but also a turquoise ring from Anne, Queen of France. It was her way of inviting the King of Scots to be her champion, her knight, and she asked that he step a pace into England and strike a blow in her cause. But this was no tournament. This was war. At home, James was advised against it by his own Queen and by the wise Bishop Elphinstone who had guided him well in the past.

James was still uncertain. On 26th July he summoned the great host of Scotland to muster at Ellem on the banks of the Whiteadder in Berwickshire. Two days later he sent his principal herald, Lyon King-of-Arms, to carry his final warning to Henry VIII at Calais. At the same time, he ordered the fleet to sea. Out of the Forth sailed the mighty *Michael* and the proud *Margaret* with their escort of smaller warships. They turned not south towards England, but north.

Henry's reply to James IV of Scotland could only have one result. He instructed the Lyon King-of-Arms to return and –

'Thus say to your master – that I am the very owner of Scotland and that he holdeth it from me by homage, and in so much as now contrary to his bounden duty, he being my vassal, doth rebel against me, with God's help I shall, at my return, expulse him from his realm, and so tell him.'

It was the old cry of English sovereignty yet again. On the 22nd August 1513, the Scottish host crossed the Tweed and struck south into England. It was the most powerful army Scotland had ever put to the field, twenty thousand strong, well armed and armoured. Apart from the usual baggage train there were seventeen great guns drawn by four hundred oxen. They were attended by gangs of workmen and supplied by powder carts and strings of pack animals laden down with gunstones. The border castles at Norham, Etal and Wark fell as, snail paced, the army crept south. By the fourth day of September, Ford Castle, barely seven miles into England, had been taken.

But another column, of equal strength, was on the move. The Earl of Surrey had raised the men of Lancashire and Yorkshire, Cheshire, Northumberland and Durham, and of the Borderlands too. Henry VIII, still in France, had left the ageing earl to guard the realm. Surrey meant to do just that.

At Alnwick on the 4th September the English army were joined by Admiral Howard with a thousand men and guns from their fleet. Less than thirty miles separated the two great forces. James was kept closely informed of the English presence by his scouts and with all castles taken his way home was clear. The Scots could now withdraw, until the English had disbanded, and then strike again. It was the Scottish way. James may even have been preparing to do just that when into the Scottish camp rode Rouge Croix, the English Herald. He presented the Scottish King with a stinging challenge to wait and do battle with the Earl of Surrey.

The English commander knew that he must bring the Scots to battle or they would raid and run as they pleased. He also knew the Scottish King could not resist a challenge. On the 6th September, James sent his Islay Herald south towards Alnwick. He informed the Earl that the Scots would wait until midday on 9th September.

The English Herald, Rouge Croix, arrives at the Scottish camp

Flodden

Surrey made all possible speed towards the Scottish lines. He found that James had positioned his army with great skill. A mile or two west of Castle Ford, and on the other side of the Till, the ground rises above the marshy carseland of the river valley to form three low hills. The most south-easterly of these is called Flodden Edge and there the Scots were arrayed, their guns menacing the only approach.

For Surrey the position was hopeless. He had issued a challenge that he could not hope to honour. He tried to tempt James once more, suggesting that the battle should be fought on open ground. James would have none of it. He refused even to receive Rouge Croix. The Scottish King sent word to Surrey that it was hardly proper for earls to choose the ground on which kings must fight. The Scots would stay where they stood.

The English now swung wide of the Scots guns and moved north, seeking a better place from which to attack. It was risky. Their undefended flank was now exposed to a charge by the Scots spearsmen. James declined. He was not going to be tempted from his hill fortress by insults, traps or anything else.

Having missed the chance to launch an attack on the passing army, James was forced to regroup his defences on the most northerly slope of the three hills, Branxton Ridge, to face Surrey in his new position.

It was late in the afternoon of Friday 9th September when the two armies confronted each other in battle readiness across a windswept quarter mile at the edge of the Cheviot Hills. Then the first real artillery barrage in history began. The Scots were soon regreting that the best of their gunners were with the fleet, many miles away. And they would regret too that their guns were so heavy. In any event it was the raking fire of the lighter and more accurate English gunnery that silenced the mighty Scots cannon.

But James could still turn the battle in his favour. He could withdraw over the Branxton Ridge and let the English soldiers make their breathless way up the steep slopes. Here they would be met by fresh Scottish spears at the crest. Instead, he chose to advance. Here he could be successful too, so long as the steady close-packed line of lowered spears held together as it flowed forward. But the ground was rough and very slippery. The steady Scottish advance became a charge, with James leading. The charge became a slithering slide, down into an unexpected valley. The slide became an uphill struggle and the huge six-metre spears of the Scots, unstoppable in tight formation, were no match for the much shorter axe-like bills of the English. The Scots drew their swords, and with desperate courage made what they could of it.

On the Scottish side the Borderers and Gordons

scattered the men of Cheshire. But they forgot the battle and went after plunder. The centre, led by the King himself came almost within reach of the Earl of Surrey who was directing his men from the rear. Then, at the very point of breaking through, James was killed. The fighting went on but the day was lost, and when darkness came the slaughter ended. As many as ten thousand Scots of all ranks including their King lay dead on Flodden Field.

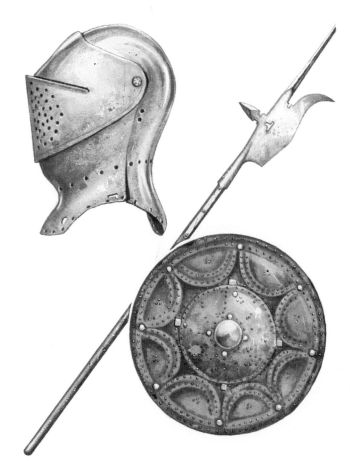

Typical weapons of the period, from **top to bottom:** English bascinet helmet; English bill; Scottish targe

A surviving Scots banner from Flodden Field

24

Worksection

A Time of Change
Understand your Work

James IV and his Land
1 How did James IV bring peace amongst the feuding nobles?
2 Where did most people live in the Scotland of James IV?
3 What kind of plough was in use on the farms?
4 Were the tenants secure on their rented farms?
5 What was bad about this arrangement?
6 What kind of houses did the country folk live in?
7 How did they spend their evenings?
8 What was a ploughgate?
9 What were the main crops in Scotland at this time?
10 What crops had to be grown by order of James I?

Farms and Farming
1 Where were the farm cottages placed?
2 How were the hillside fields fertilised?
3 What system was used for cropping the infield?
4 How was the farm land divided so that each family received its fair share of the good and poor soil?
5 Why were Scottish fields not as long and not as straight as those in England?
6 How were enough oxen provided to pull the heavy plough?
7 A fair system was used for ploughing the strips of field belonging to the various farmers. How did this work?
8 Did these farmers work as a team all the year round?
9 Apart from milk and meat what did the flocks and herds provide?

Burghs and Burgh Life
1 Why were the burghs unhealthy places to live?
2 In what ways was a burgh a kind of club?
3 What was the main purpose of the burghs?
4 Did the townsfolk give up farming altogether?
5 How often did markets take place?
6 Apart from buying and selling what else happened in the market places?
7 What happened because of the filthy conditions in the burghs?
8 How did the authorities try to control this?
9 About how many burghs were seaports?
10 What did Scotland export and import through her seaports?
11 Did the seaports serve any purpose apart from trade?
12 Was the fishing fleet used only for fishing?

Medicine, Education and Printing
1 Which was the first university in Britain to have a medical school?
2 Why was this not as helpful as it might have been?
3 Who provided the more useful type of medical care?
4 What organisation did they form?
5 What was it they had the sole right to sell?
6 What else did James give them the right to?
7 How did Scotland's first Education Act help to spread education?
8 Why was James so keen to improve education?
9 What penalty did he lay down for those who disobeyed the Education Act?
10 Where and by whom was Scotland's first printing press set up?
11 What books did they print?

James's Wedding
1 Whom did James IV marry?
2 How did he test the strength of his laws?
3 What did people say of James's bridge?
4 In what way was the poet William Dunbar not being strictly honest about the wedding?
5 In what way was James not being strictly honest in celebrating his wedding so richly?

Construction
1 Where did James construct a new palace?
2 What palaces did he extend?
3 What castles did he repair and rebuild?
4 How did James prepare for the building of his new fleet?
5 What was the fleet for?
6 What was the name of James's first real man of war? How many guns did it have?
7 What was his most powerful ship?
8 How did he test the strength of his great new warship?

Trouble with England
1 How was James being forced into war with England?
2 What message was sent to him from France?
3 What name was given to the treaty between France and Scotland?
4 What insult finally stung James into action against the English?
5 What sort of army did James lead?
6 How well was the Scottish army positioned before the Battle of Flodden?
7 How did James reply when the Earl of Surrey sent Rouge Croix to challenge him a second time?
8 What early chance of success did James miss?
9 Where were the best Scottish gunners?
10 How did James err for the second time?
11 What upset the Scottish advance?
12 How did James's position on the battlefield differ from the Earl of Surrey's?

Use Your Imagination

1 Why do you think short leases did not encourage the Scottish farmers to develop their farms?

2 Why, do you suppose, was ploughing done as a team while the other farming activities were done independently?

3 What might suggest that the Scottish farming system was not too unsuccessful?

4 Why was life on the farms healthier than in the burghs?

5 Why were nearby farmers required to sell their produce in the burgh market?

6 What was it, do you think, that the burgh folk did not understand about disease that caused them to keep the burghs as they were?

7 Why was a fishing fleet particularly useful to the King?

8 Why did James arrange for the College of Surgeons to have a criminal's corpse each year?

9 How did James change the Scottish royal court? What sort of people did he include?

10 Why do you think Scotland in James IV time was so unwilling to go to war with England?

11 Why do you suppose the Scots did not lead the English Army on a hopeless chase as they had done in the past? Why do you think they stood and fought a pitched battle?

Further Work

1 Square rigged ships like the *Michael* had their sails hung on yard arms. Make this little test model and see what your group can find out about how they were rigged. You will need –

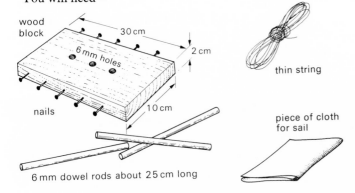

wood block

30 cm

2 cm

6 mm holes

10 cm

nails

thin string

piece of cloth for sail

6 mm dowel rods about 25 cm long

The Mast

A Put a dowel in one of the holes. This is the mast of your ship. When the sails fill they will pull on the mast and make it bend, like this

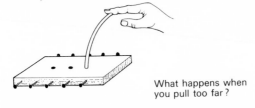

What happens when you pull too far?

B Now put up a new mast!

Your group's job is to prevent the mast bending and breaking using the string, just like the guy ropes on a tent pole. But REMEMBER the sails have to hang at the front of the mast and must not get tangled up in the shrouds (the ropes that hold the mast). Of course the mast is never bent backwards by the sails.

The Sails

Now that your mast is properly supported you can add a sail. First attach your sail to a piece of dowel and then attach the dowel to the mast, like this –

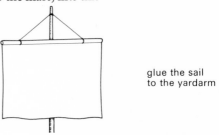

glue the sail to the yardarm

Think about these ideas and, as you do, add more ropes to your sail to improve your control of it –

1 The sail has to be held at the bottom to catch the wind.

2 You should be able to turn and hold the yard-arm to face the sail in the right direction.

3 You should be able to furl the sail when it is not required.

When your ship is fully rigged, compare your design with the *Michael* on page 21. Put your model on display to the rest of the class with notes to explain how it works.

2 Jean Elliot, an 18th century poet, wrote about the Battle of Flodden in a poem called 'The Flowers of the Forest'. In one verse she said –

> Dule and wae for the order sent our lads to the Border;
> The English, for once, by guile won the day;
> The Flowers of the Forest, that foucht aye the foremost
> The prime o' our land, are cauld in the clay.

It is published in the *Oxford Book of Scottish Verse*. Try to find a copy to read and enjoy.

3 Imagine that you are standing somewhere by a harbour at sunset when the sky to the west is tinged with red. The harbour wall and the sailing ships are black against the sun. The masts and rigging make patterns you would not see by daylight. Here is a way to paint such a scene.

A First prepare a background of sky and harbour wall. A good way to paint the sky is to use very wet paint and then to add clouds by dripping darker paint on the wet surface.
Make the top half of your sky from cool grey blue shades and the lower part from pale oranges and reds.

B When the background is *completely dry*, paint a black harbour wall across the bottom of the picture and add the top part of a sailing ship's hull showing above the wall – also black.

C Now, when everything is quite dry use a black fibre tip pen to add masts with all the rigging to hold them firm. Then draw yard-arms with all the ropes to control them. The more rigging and ropes you *carefully* draw the better your picture will be – but you should know what all the ropes are for!

4 Try to trace on a map the route followed by James's army on its way to Flodden. Find also where the English army was coming from. Make your own map of the movements described on pages 23 and 24.

The Fifth James

After the battle

In the closing months of 1513 all Scotland ached with the pain of Flodden. So great was the loss and suffering throughout the land that for many years no one would mention the battle by name. Yet few in this stubborn little kingdom of the north thought it a proper end to the war. This was not the first time, nor would it be the last, that Scots had braced themselves against the shockwave of crushing defeat. And there was still the spring to come when the frozen ground would thaw and a new army would be raised.

Defence measures

In Edinburgh, though its provost had fallen in the battle, the Town Council met in urgent session. They ordered the immediate building of a city wall to protect the capital and they instructed women not to wail in the streets and spread despair. They were to seek comfort in the church and there pray for aid. A town watch of twenty-four men was formed to mount guard on the city. The Lords of the High Council organised the re-arming of the people against invasion, and gathered weapons and equipment from wherever they could be found.

A new king

On the 21st September, 1513, less than a fortnight after the disaster at Flodden Field, James V was crowned King of Scots in the Chapel Royal of Stirling Castle. He was barely seventeen months old. For all the rich splendour of the ceremony, it was remembered as the Mourning Coronation. The death of King James IV, and so many others, at the foot of Branxton Ridge cast a long and sombre shadow over any celebration; his reckless gallantry would yet cost his nation dearly.

Surrey did not invade. His own army had suffered harshly and his king was still in France. It is unlikely too, that Henry VIII would thank his Earl for being too successful. It would never do for ageing Surrey to outshine his royal lord. In any case, England's war was with France, and Scotland was not likely to be too troublesome, at least for the time being.

Whatever the reason for the delay it gave the Scots time to organise the government of the realm. As required by James IV's will, Queen Margaret was made regent to rule in their son's name. But that was only until she married again, which she did within the year. In 1515, the Duke of Albany arrived from France to be Guardian of the Realm.

The coronation of James V

The Duke of Albany

Albany ruled well and wisely from 1515–1524, or at least during the years he was in Scotland. He twice returned to France during this time. The first visit, in 1517, was to renew the Auld Alliance, but because the French king had made a treaty with England, Albany was kept in France until 1521. While he was away the principal families in the land made their bid for power – Red Douglases against Hamiltons. It was decided finally in the High Street of Edinburgh with sword and pike. Douglas won but the people of the city had the last word. They called the affair 'Cleanse the Causeway,' and so passed their own judgment on those who took part. In Edinburgh, cleansing the causeway was a mucky business, removing the filth and rubbish that gathered there.

Albany returned in November 1521, as the new Anglo-French friendship had already gone sour. The Duke was encouraged to stir up trouble for the English – more border raiding, even invasion. But the memory of Flodden was too fresh. The Scots were not willing to risk everything just to suit France.

In 1522, Albany went back to France and in his absence the English struck at Scotland. Henry VIII sent the Duke of Norfolk, son of Flodden's Earl of Surrey, to burn and plunder. Again the borderland was wasted – crops and trees, villages and towers. Kelso was burned at the height of that summer. Jedburgh too was put to the torch. Albany returned with a force of men and guns from France and with the Scots drove the English out. But still the Scottish nobles would not cross the border. There was little Albany could do to help the French cause in Scotland so he sailed back to France in the May of 1524 and there remained. The nobles were loose once more, Hamiltons and Douglases greedy for power and personal gain.

Portrait of the Duke of Albany and Margaret Tudor

Jedburgh burning at the hands of the men of the Duke of Norfolk

A Douglas as Guardian

Again the Red Douglases had the best of it. Archibald Douglas, Earl of Angus became Guardian. Every important post in the kingdom was filled by members of the family. In Edinburgh Castle, as captive of Angus since November 1525, lay the forgotten boy, James V, King of Scotland. All power belonged to the Earl of Angus and no one dared move against him while he held the boy king hostage (*see caption*).

James arrived at Stirling at the end of May 1528. When confused rumours of the King's escape reached the Douglases they at once rode in force on the castle. They were prevented by a Royal Herald who read the King's proclamation forbidding any Douglas to come within six miles of the Royal Person. And James continued in the way he had begun. With a modest army he soon had Angus under siege in Tantallon Castle near North Berwick. When the Earl surrendered in November he was banished with his kin from the realm. They were welcomed in England by James's uncle.

James takes control

James V could begin to rule his kingdom. Again the first task was to restore law and order. In 1530, he marched through the borders where the Armstrongs of Liddesdale boasted their contempt for kings whether English or Scottish and raided as they pleased. And there were others too almost as bad – The Earls of Home and Bothwell, the Maxwells and Scotts and more. Not only did James need to enforce law and order, he had to make sure also that the wild behaviour of these lordly ruffians gave Henry no reason to break the truce and attack Scotland yet again. John Armstrong and forty of his men were hanged. Others were thrown in prison.

James also brought the Highlands and Islands to obedience. Soon, throughout the realm, the King's Peace was kept. Kings who bring peace to the daily lives of the common folk are liked by their people. James was the 'Poor Man's King'. He would disguise himself as a humble tenant farmer and roam the countryside in search of experience and adventure.

There is a story, though the truth of it is uncertain, that in the spring of 1528 the young James was being held at Falkland Palace in Fife. He was a boy of sixteen by then. Late one evening he told James Douglas of Parkhead, who was in charge of the royal captive while Angus was away on other business, that he planned a hunting trip the following day. James then retired to bed reminding his warder that it would be an early start. There never was a hunting trip nor was there ever meant to be. At dead of night James stole from his rooms disguised as a Yeoman of the Stable and left the castle unrecognised on a fast horse. He rode furiously for Stirling Castle where his mother, Queen Margaret, had made arrangements for him to be received.

Far and wide, the poor man's king was known by the nickname the Gudeman o' Ballengreich; his disguise fooled nobody, and pleased everybody.

The King's marriage

On New Year's Day 1537, at Notre Dame Cathedral in Paris, James married the Princess Madeleine of France. On the 19th May he arrived at Leith with his new Queen and a large dowry. Queen Madeleine, a frail and tender creature, stepped on the Scottish shore and knelt to kiss the soil of her new kingdom. Sadly she was too delicate to survive the harshness of this northern land and she died within two brief months of her arrival. In less than a year however, James was married again, this time to Mary of Guise who brought an even larger dowry.

With dowry payments and Church taxes the royal coffers began to overflow. James spent freely on his palaces and royal splendour, more perhaps than all the James's that went before. And as he grew older, he grew greedier and more cruel. The ruthless justice he imposed became a reign of terror under a harsh tyrant. Not only did the nobles live in fear of their lives, particularly if their wealth would pass to the King on their deaths, but lesser men suffered cruelly also. A thief was burnt at the stake and two men were drawn, hung and beheaded at his command. This severity was rare in Scotland – but then James was half Tudor, through his mother. His uncle was Henry VIII. England's future queen, Bloody Mary, was James's full cousin. More than Stewart blood flowed richly in the veins of the Scottish King.

By twice choosing a French queen, James had made it clear enough that he meant to keep the Auld Alliance. This came badly for Henry VIII at a time when he faced trouble from abroad. By taking control of the Church in England from the Pope, Henry had gained great wealth from Monasteries and Abbeys. But he had set England against powerful countries like France and the Empire states that were faithful to Rome. A great crusade against England was planned and James had promised to take part. Henry did his best to get James to do with the Church in Scotland as he had done in the south, telling him of the riches that he would gain. The Scottish King replied that he could have what he wanted from his Church simply by asking. There would be no need to do more.

The nave of Notre Dame Cathedral, Paris

Coat of arms of France and Scotland

Negotiations with Henry VIII

But things changed. By 1541 the great crusade had been forgotten in the quarrels of the main partners. Now each wanted Henry's help against the other. Henry felt safer and stronger. He looked to the north once more and invited James to meet him at York. James appeared to agree. For the first time in his reign the English King travelled to York, where he expected to get the results he wanted. James's advisers suspected that Henry would simply kidnap the Scottish king and proclaim himself overlord of Scotland. After twelve days of waiting Henry, embarrassed and enraged returned to London.

Portrait of King Henry VIII of England

Coat of arms of
the Duke of Norfolk

Henry's revenge

In the August of that year, Henry turned loose his northern army on the Borderland. When the Earl of Huntly scattered the invaders at Haddonrig in Teviotdale, Henry blamed the Scots for the trouble and sent another army to punish them! This time it was led by the Duke of Norfolk who met little resistance. The borderlands were looted and wasted, Kelso and Roxburgh plundered and burned. But Norfolk had his own problems of supply and turned south again with his hungry army.

But this war was not popular with the Scots and James himself was to blame. He had lost the trust and support of the nobles by his harsh treatment. The King was believed to have a death list of more than three hundred noblemen who could be tried for heresy or treason, whenever he chose. The host that mustered to James' standard on the burgh muir of Edinburgh

Portrait of James V

were uneasy and unwilling. They marched south-east to Fala Muir, fourteen or so miles from the capital and there learned that Norfolk had returned to England.

A month later, at the head of his new army, James struck south-west towards the Solway, determined to cross into England. On that uneasy march James became ill and had to retire to Lochmaben castle, leaving Oliver Sinclair to carry on the unwilling invasion.

At Solway Moss on 24th November, a small force of Englishmen, no more than three thousand strong, boldly faced the dispirited Scots. There was no real battle. Too many Scots were ready to surrender rather than risk death for a King in whom they had no trust. Twelve hundred prisoners were taken and the rest of James's army melted into the grey November hills.

Death of James V

The news was brought to the Scottish King at Lochmaben. Sick at heart he rode wearily and aimlessly to Edinburgh, then to Linlithgow where his queen was soon to have their child. After a week he went on to Falkland Palace where he took to his bed. There he heard of the birth of his baby daughter. In the blackness of his despair, and perhaps because his two baby sons had died, he believed she would not survive. He said simply, 'It came with a lass (Marjory Bruce) and it will pass with a lass,' and turned his face to the wall. He died a week later on 14th December, only thirty-one, but worn out in spirit like an old tired man. He was remembered by his nobles as a tyrant and by the common people as the poor man's king – the Gudeman o' Ballengreich. He was both.

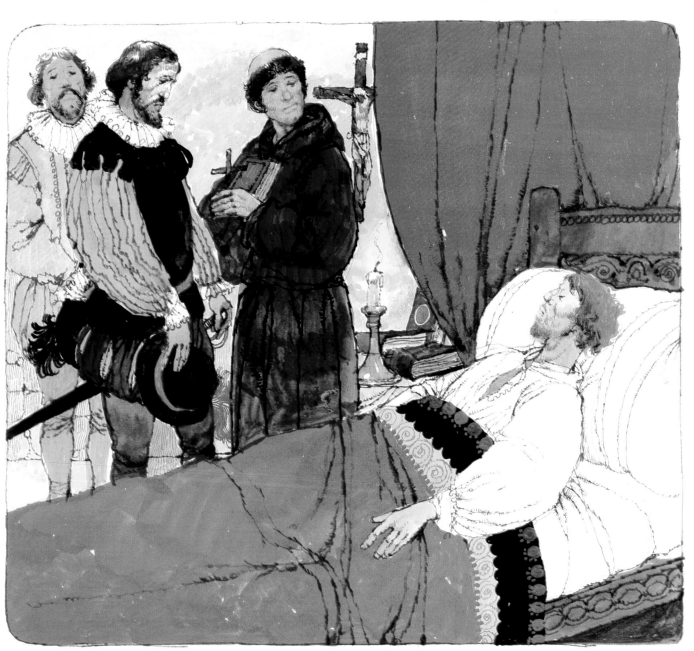

Worksection

The Fifth James
Understand Your Work

After Flodden
1 Did the Scots feel that the defeat at Flodden meant they had lost the war?
2 When did they expect to renew the conflict?
3 What steps were taken to protect Edinburgh against invasion?
4 At what age was James V crowned?
5 Why was it remembered as the mourning coronation?
6 What reasons could the Earl of Surrey have had for not invading Scotland immediately after Flodden?
7 How did this delay help the Scots?

The Duke of Albany
1 Who ruled Scotland for the Infant King?
2 Why did the Duke of Albany visit France in 1517?
3 Why was he detained there?
4 How did this affect Scotland?
5 How was the struggle for power settled between the Red Douglases and the Hamiltons?
6 What did the common people think of this struggle?
7 Why were the Scots unwilling to start up the border raiding when the Duke of Albany returned from France?
8 Who helped the Scots to drive out the English invaders, led by the Earl of Norfolk?
9 Why did the Duke of Albany return to France in 1524? What started again when he left?

A Douglas as Guardian
1 Who became Guardian of Scotland after Albany?
2 How did he make sure he held all the power?
3 How is it thought that the boy king, James V, managed to escape from Falkland Palace?
4 How did he prevent the Douglases capturing him again after his escape?
5 What did James V do with the Earl of Angus and his family when he defeated them?
6 Who welcomed the Earl and his family?

James Rules
1 How did James enforce the law in the borders?
2 Why was he very anxious to bring order in that part of the country?
3 Where else did he restore order?
4 How was he regarded by the common folk?
5 Were people deceived by James's disguise?
6 What was the nickname they gave him?

The King's marriage
1 Where and when was James V first married?
2 In what month did his wife die?
3 Who was his second wife?
4 How did his marriage affect the wealth of the crown?
5 What did James do with his money?
6 How did he change as he grew older?

7 How did James show that he meant to keep the Auld Alliance?
8 Why did James not like Henry VIII's suggestion that he too make himself head of the church?

James and Henry VIII
1 Why did James not keep his appointment with Henry VIII in York?
2 How did Henry avenge himself on James for failing to meet him in York?
3 What caused the Scottish nobles to fear and distrust James V?
4 How did this affect his campaign against England?
5 What happened to James on his march to the Solway to invade England?
6 What happened to the invasion?

Death of James V
1 How did James react to the news from Solway?
2 How did he receive the news of the birth of his daughter?
3 Did James think his daughter would live to be Queen?
4 What did the nobles think of James?
5 How did the people remember this King?

Use Your Imagination

1 Why do you think the Town Council of Edinburgh forbade the women to weep and wail in the streets after the Battle of Flodden?

2 In what way might James IV have been missed after his death? What new developments might stop then?

3 What was it about James V that the ordinary people liked?

4 Why do you suppose Henry VIII was so anxious to get James to take over the Church just as Henry had done in England? How could this help Henry?

5 Why do you think James V's nobles were so unwilling to risk their lives fighting the English?

6 What did James mean when he said 'It came with a lass and it will pass with a lass'?

Further Work

1 Imagine you are living in Edinburgh just after the Battle of Flodden and you keep a diary. Think about what you would write on Monday 12th September, when news of the disaster at Flodden has reached Edinburgh. How are the people behaving? What is the Town Council doing? How do you feel? What do you fear might happen? Now make a note of the entry in your diary.

2 King James V put down the unruly border nobles and hanged one called Johnnie Armstrong along with twenty-

four of his men. There is a balled about this event which you can read in the *Oxford Book of Ballads* (page 398).

3   Here is a way your class can 'build' a great ship like the '*Michael*' which was sold to the French during James V early years. Just as in real ship building, there are different jobs to be done – hull building, mast making, rigging and sailmaking and so on. And you will need materials and tools – wood-coloured paper to build from and paste and scissors to work with.

The picture on page 21 will help you with your design.

Hull Builders

Materials – a large background sheet pinned to the wall at working height; strips of paper for your elm keel and oak ribs, oak planking and pine decks; paste and scissors.

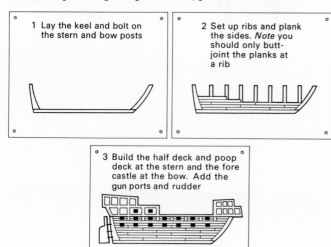

The planks on your ship are laid edge to edge – carvel fashion and not overlapped. The gaps between need to be filled (caulked) with rope and tar. You fill your seams with black felt pen. When you are satisfied that the hull is complete and watertight cut it out from the backing paper ready for launching.

Mast Makers

Materials – long straight strips of paper, tapering like tall fir trees, paste and scissors.

There are four masts to be made and a bowsprit.

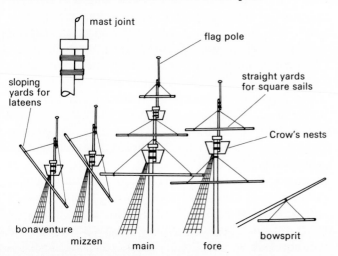

The Main mast is the tallest and its made taller by adding two parts – top and gallant. The others have top masts added.

Make your masts and yards and add crow's nests where the joins are.

When the hull is launched add the masts, and rig them using either brown string stuck on or felt pen.

Sail Makers

Materials. White paper or cloth, glue and scissors, brushes and paints. Make your sails to fit the yards like this

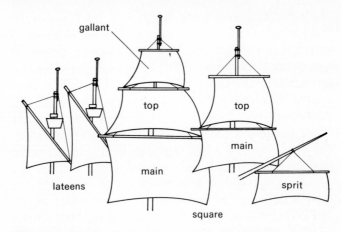

When your sails are ready make flags and pennants for your mastheads and elsewhere on the ship – Lion Rampants, St Andrew's Crosses and so on. Add sails and flags when the ship is launched and getting under way.

Sea Makers

Materials – large background paper pinned to the wall at working height; paints, large brushes, scissors, glue, coloured magazine paper. Make a place for your ship to sail, something like this.

First paint the sky, hills and sea. Then build the harbour wall with stone coloured paper and add people waving, and bollards etc. Cut a slit in the sea to allow the hull to settle into the water.

A New Church

The Greenwich Agreement

With the death of James V, Scotland remembered Alexander III who, thrown from his horse, had died leaving the infant Margaret of Norway to be the Scottish Queen. Now in 1542 James had left his infant daughter Mary to be Queen of Scots. Margaret's closest male relative had been Great Uncle Edward I, King of England and Hammer of the Scots. Now, Mary's nearest kinsman was Great Uncle Henry VIII, King of England and no less a 'hammer'. Edward I had had a boy prince, who should have married Margaret in order to secure the Scottish throne. Now Henry VIII's son was to marry Mary and follow the same path. Edward's plan failed, but now, two and a half centuries later, Henry would take care not to let it fail a second time.

But fail it did, and for much the same reasons. At first things went well enough. At Greenwich, on the 1st July 1543, a treaty was signed by which Prince Edward would be married to Mary when she was eleven. Until then there would be peace. Henry wanted more, of course, much more. He wanted possession of Mary, a kind of royal hostage and the end of the Auld Alliance with France. He wanted to be Lord Superior of Scotland. He wanted English garrisons to hold the major Scottish castles. Like Edward I, he wanted to swallow Scotland whole. The Greenwich agreement might not have been a bad start had Henry been more patient.

Portrait of Edward VII

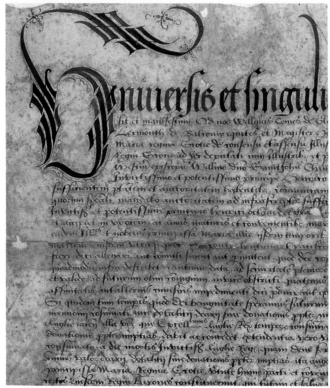

The Treaty of Greenwich (detail)

The Church of Rome

Many people were no longer satisfied with the way in which the mighty Church of Rome conducted its affairs. Plain folk in the burghs and farms of Scotland, where plague, famine and poverty hung darkly over their daily lives, found it hard to understand the luxury and wealth enjoyed by some bishops and abbots while church buildings leaked and crumbled, and parish priests were too few, too poor and uneducated. The hand of the Church that once reached out to people in need, was now more grasping than giving. The poor often paid for a christian burial with their best clothes or second best animal – the upmaist cloth or the kirk cow. Greed born of need made penniless priests demand offerings from penniless folk. For a fee they would sometimes even pronounce an excommunication (the worst kind of holy curse) by request, against anyone, however slight the offence, real or imagined. Such church services as the people could attend were in Latin and often stuttered and stumbled over by a priest who understood little of the language or its purpose. It was a poor kind of worship for common folk.

'in commendam'

From the time of James III, abbeys and priories were being given in trust, 'in commendam' to people, not necessarily churchmen. At first the idea was to protect the abbey while a new abbot was chosen. The reward received was the monies collected by the abbey during the period of protection. Now 'commendations', as they were called, were handed out by the king to secure favour and support, and they were life-long. Now many bishops, sons of nobles and the like, held their posts 'in commendam' and were not men of the Church at all. Paisley had a ten year old abbot, who was the nephew of the Archbishop of St Andrews and there was a fourteen year old at the Abbey of Deer in Aberdeenshire. The money drawn by the Church was passing into the hands of nobles and not being used to help the needy and spread the gospel.

Church buildings

Devout and faithful members of the Church at all levels saw it was sorely in need of repair. Parliament itself complained of the 'unhonesty and misrule of kirkmen'. An archbishop reported that church buildings were in ruin, without glass in the windows and on the verge of collapse; that people were unable to hear divine services and the Mass celebrated. They were even without fonts for christenings. Cardinal Sermoneta, having investigated the state of the Church in Scotland reported urgently to the Pope.

Protestants

There were others, devout Catholics, who believed that the fault ran deeper. They protested that even where it was working as it should, the Church had come too far from Christ. They protested too that there could be only one head of the Church, not the Pope, not the King as now in England, but Christ and Christ alone. They protested that the way people lived was the important thing in the salvation of their souls. These protesters or 'protestants' as they were called, were declaring that the Church itself needed change, not simply repair. They were teaching a new word, preaching for a New Church in which they sincerely believed.

A sixteenth century gold rosary

In Germany, Martin Luther had set men's minds ablaze, declaring that 'if a Christian has faith he has everything.' His words and his message came to Scotland by the trade routes. And people listened and wondered. They listened in the burghs where they had supported their own churches and priests for a very long time with little enough help from great bishops. They wondered, since they had managed without bishops, did they need the Pope or the Mass? Perhaps Luther's way should be their way.

But there were still others who saw how a change might be used to their own benefit. There were nobles eager to grab the lands and wealth of abbeys and monasteries. There were kings and emperors who saw profit and glory in turning the Church against those of another faith, always to save their souls and usually by breaking their bodies!

Scotland was adrift in a storm tossed sea with an infant hand on the helm. The country boiled as the new ideas of Luther and John Calvin were roared from pulpits and in the streets and in the fields. And the greater nation states of France and England plotted and struggled, each to have Scotland for her own. As always there was the struggle of powerful men over the royal cradle. This time, because there were large numbers of people interested in a new religion, support could be sought in England, which had rejected Rome. Henry jumped at the chance. In 1543 he sent north Archibald Douglas, Earl of Angus, with ten Scottish lords taken willing captive at Solway Moss. James Hamilton, Earl of Arran, almost a Protestant, became Guardian of the Realm to rule in the little Mary's name until she was of age. His main rival, Cardinal Beaton, Archbishop of St Andrews, found himself locked up in various castles, the last one being his own. He favoured the Catholic side of France, seeing the real danger of Scotland being swallowed up by England. Henry had done well.

But then he did badly. He had managed in July 1543 at Greenwich to get agreement for Mary's future marriage to the Prince of Wales. Now he started insisting again on all the other things he wanted – Mary to be held in England, himself to be Lord Superior, English garrisons in Scottish castles and an end to the Auld Alliance. For a great many Scots, even on the Protestant side, this was too much. The Archbishop freed himself and, the support of the Queen Mother forced the regent Arran to change sides. The Scottish Parliament then threw out the treaty. All that Henry had gained was lost.

Portrait of John Calvin

Portrait of Martin Luther

Henry attacks Edinburgh

At first Henry had tried to bribe the Scottish nobles. Scotland with French aid was able to pay larger bribes and so the nobles, interested as always in themselves, stayed 'loyal'. When that plan failed Henry showed his true feelings by sending the Earl of Hertford and a powerful army north to 'turne upset downe the Cardinalles town of St Andrews, … sparing no creature alyve within the same.'

It was May 1544 when the huge fleet carrying Hertford's army rounded the Bass Rock and entered the Firth of Forth. It was clearly seen from the height of Edinburgh Castle but both the Earl of Arran and the Cardinal in whose hands Scotland's safekeeping lay, thought it must be a returning fishing fleet. All Edinburgh went about their Sunday business in peace. The attack was as devastating as it was surprising. It was this city and not St Andrews that they burned and looted. Holyrood Palace was destroyed. The sky over Stirling's plain was darkened with the smoke of burning towns and villages. Men, women and children were butchered to satisfy Henry's rage. And in the south, a second army destroyed the lovely border abbeys at Kelso and Dryburgh, Melrose and Jedburgh. Though the crops they burnt would grow again the wondrous abbeys were never to be rebuilt. Hertford and his henchmen moved south leaving a trail of death and destruction from Leith to the border. He returned the next year for more.

The slaughter of women and children, the wasting of town and country, the plunder and destruction of cattle, crops and mills drove the people into the arms of France. Now Protestants were thought of as people who supported Henry VIII. Now Cardinal Beaton turned against these 'reformers of the Church.' Opposing the Catholic Church was opposing France, and opposing France was supporting England. Heresy, which means religious ideas that differ from those of the Catholic Church, was now the same as treason.

The infant Queen's mother, Mary of Guise, was French. Cardinal Beaton was head of the Catholic Church in Scotland. Both had good reason to hate the new Church and its threat to their religion and the Auld Alliance. Now that the Regent Arran had weakened his support for the Protestants, the Queen Mother and the Cardinal set about crushing the new religion. They meant to keep Scotland true to the Old Church and close to France. England would not swallow Scotland. But now there was a danger that France might.

Henry's brutal attacks in 1544 and 1545 had turned Cardinal Beaton more fiercely against heresy. The new preachers were burned at the stakes in St Andrews, Edinburgh, and Glasgow. But these fires kindled an even stronger yearning amongst pious men for this new faith which promised to fill their lives. They were driven before the Cardinal's flames to seek refuge with Scotland's enemy in the south, which suited King Henry fine.

Hertford's fleet rounding Bass Rock

Patrick Hamilton

Cardinal Beaton would have done better had he remembered the advice given to his uncle when he ordered the burning of Patrick Hamilton in 1528. When threatened with the stake and ordered to deny his new faith, Patrick Hamilton said simply, 'I will rather be content that my body burn in this fire for confessing my faith in Christ, than it burn in the fire of Hell for denying the same.'

It took six long tortured hours for Patrick Hamilton to die in a smouldering St Andrews fire which windswept rain had damped on that bleak day in February. Those who watched were astounded at his patient endurance. The young martyr did more for the new faith by his dying than he could ever have done in his life. The Archbishop was warned then that any more such burnings would spread the new beliefs for 'the reek of Master Patrick Hamilton had infected as many as it blew upon.' It infected many more than that. A faith for which a man would so suffer attracted many new followers. The Archbishop's nephew would now make the same mistake again.

A woodcut from Holinshed's 'Chronicles', depicting the execution of George Wishart

George Wishart

George Wishart had been a teacher in Montrose Grammar School in 1538 when he came under suspicion of heresy for using a Greek New Testament. He left the country hurriedly. Now, in 1544, he was back and preaching more loudly than before. He had studied the teachings of John Calvin in Switzerland and had also spent time at Cambridge. His new preaching won converts to the Protestant faith and new friends for the English King. Henry had made sure that Wishart's time in Cambridge had not been wasted. Cardinal Beaton saw Wishart as a danger to the Old Church and an agent of England.

In the January of 1546, George Wishart was arrested on charges of heresy while preaching in Haddington with a young local man whose own voice would one day sound loudly in the same cause. His name was John Knox.

Wishart was taken for trial to St Andrews. There on 1st March, at a stake before the Cardinal's Palace, he was strangled and his body burned for the crime of heresy. From a nearby window Beaton watched unmoved as George Wishart kissed in forgiveness the cheeks of his executioner. Others were more impressed by his pious courage. The Cardinal had forgotten Patrick Hamilton, and the Protestant faith grew strong again. From the same window, not two months later, hung the lifeless body of Cardinal Beaton. He had been stabbed to death in his castle on the morning of 29th May after a brief invitation at swordpoint to 'repent the shedding of Wishart's blood.'

Yet again the savagery rebounded against those who committed it. The Fife lairds who had avenged Wishart found themselves without support. They seized the castle of St Andrews and held it for a year against the feeble siege of the Earl of Arran, once more restored to power by the death of Beaton.

Henry VIII died in the following January 1547, but that had little effect. Hertford now became Duke of Somerset and Protector of England, regent for the boy king, Edward VI. Some thought that the English might come to the aid of the fugitives in St Andrews. Perhaps for that reason, John Knox joined them there on the 10th April. He confidently began his preaching in the parish church. But it was the French and not the English who came and blasted through the walls of the castle.

Never over-popular with the Scots, the French were not asked to stay; just to remove the killers and their supporters to France for punishment. There the better born of the Wishart's avengers were imprisoned and the lesser folk, for lesser crimes, were sent to be galley slaves. Until 1549 John Knox was chained to his oar in the creaking hull of a French galley, under the cruel whip of the overseer.

The death of Cardinal Beaton

Marriage demands

England tried once more to win Mary's hand for Edward. This time they claimed to be freeing the Scots from bondage to the Pope. Protector Somerset crossed the border with sixteen thousand men and pushed towards Edinburgh. He brought six thousand cavalry, almost a thousand musketeers and a cannon train of fifteen guns with their supplies. This mighty force was supported by a fleet which tacked north along Scotland's eastern coastline.

Black Saturday

Regent Arran mustered Scotland's host to meet the invasion a little inland and to the east of Musselburgh, at a place called Pinkie. On Saturday 10th September, 1547, he drew up his army in four divisions behind the narrow River Esk. To the left was the Firth of Forth and on the right soft marshy ground offered protection. From there he watched as Protector Somerset wheeled his great column onto its battlefront. Off shore he could see the men-of-war of the English fleet nose gently into the mouth of the Esk.

Somerset won a crushing victory on Black Saturday at Pinkie but he won nothing else. Certainly not the hand of Mary in royal marriage. This rough wooing had been a disaster and a failure. No Scots believed that there had ever been any truth in the story about freeing them from the Pope. It was always too clear that the English meant not to unite the Kingdoms through marriage, but to conquer Scotland. Somerset's brutal invasion turned the Scots once more to France. In July 1584, (at the request of the Queen Mother) the French help came, seven thousand battle hardened troops.

Though the Scots outnumbered the invaders and held the stronger position, they were not nearly so well equipped with little cavalry and no real fire power, except their few Argyll bowmen. The deafening broadsides that boomed out from the Protectors fleet scattered the archers and broke up the Scottish left flank. On the right the Earl of Angus's division boldly attempted to cut off Somerset's cavalry as it made to gain the high ground. Instead the Scots found themselves struggling up to face the crushing downhill charges of the English heavy horse. For a time the schiltrons held with stubborn courage but the axe-like bill of the English foot-soldiers proved, as it did at Flodden, a better weapon than the long Scots spear. The next charge smashed through the spear rings and the whole Scots force retreated before the crashing volleys of the advancing muskets. The ranks broke and the battle was lost, but the slaughter went on. Then Leith was taken and Holyrood Abbey plundered. The great guns of the fleet now trained their mighty broadsides on Dundee. And this time when the English returned south they placed garrisons in castles wherever possible. Haddington was left very heavily manned and fortified.

above: A letter from Edward VI of England (9 years old at the time) to his uncle and regent, the Duke of Somerset, welcoming the news of the Battle of Pinkie

Portrait of Henry II of France

Typical weapons of the period, from **top to bottom:** Cast-iron cannon; English pike; arquebus; Scottish claymore

A French marriage

It was now France's turn to pounce. She demanded a future marriage between Mary Queen of Scots and the heir to the French throne. Scotland was saved from England. Now she would fall prey to France instead. The five year old Mary was shipped out to her new home at the French royal court, and there was little Scotland could do about it. It pleased her French mother, Mary of Guise, but few others who lived in this northern kingdom. It certainly pleased Henry II of France because Mary Queen of Scots was also a claimant to the English throne and Edward VI was already seriously ill. France might soon hold England too and restore the Catholic Church there. So sure of this was the French King that in 1549 he set free the prisoners taken from St Andrews Castle. John Knox made his way, not yet to his homeland, but to England and then Geneva, where he would spend the next five years.

Mary of Guise

By 1554 Mary of Guise was the sole Regent of Scotland, the Earl of Arran having been persuaded to accept a rich dukedom in France. Now this Queen-Regent began her business of making Scotland as French as she dared. She appointed her countrymen to high offices. She brought in French troops to form a regular standing army and taxed the people to pay for it. Castles were garrisoned with French troops, and she even planned an invasion of England.

The year before the Queen Mother became Regent, the young and sickly Edward VI died, and Mary Tudor, a devout Catholic, became Queen of England. At once she began the cruel persecution of the Protestant Church that was to earn her the title 'Bloody Mary'. Hundreds of pious men suffered death at the stake during her short reign. There was no longer refuge in England for Scottish Protestants and for a time the Queen-Regent had it her own way. She was able to restore the Catholic Church and maintain the Auld Alliance.

In France, in April 1558, Mary Queen of Scots, married Francis the Dauphin. In England the following November the 'Bloody Mary' died and Protestant Elizabeth was queen. No sooner was Elizabeth on the English throne than Francis and Mary now King and Queen of Scotland and soon to be King and Queen of France declared themselves King and Queen of England and Ireland too. France was ready to take over not only Scotland but England too. The French King's plan for an all Catholic Europe ruled by France was taking shape. Mary of Guise was ready to play her part. The persecution of the Protestants began again. This time the new Church of Scotland would be crushed and those who preached its message would be banished from the land.

Portrait of Mary of Guise   Mary Tudor

Many Protestants were burnt at the stake during Mary Tudor's reign

The Covenant of the 'Godlie Band', 1557

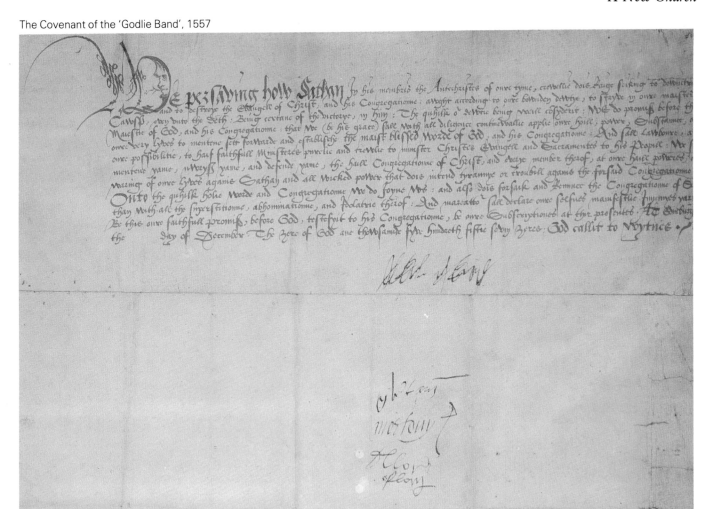

The Covenant

But the new faith would not be so easily put down. As early as December 1557 five Protestant lords called themselves the Lords of the Congregation of Jesus Christ and put their names to a Covenant which bound them to 'apply our whole power, substance and our very lives, to maintain, set forward and establish the most blessed word of God.' This 'Godlie Band' drew to itself more and more supporters. Soon it became a powerful group, excited by the holy words of the New Church, and with an eye on the rich lands of the Old.

Walter Myln

On the last day in April 1558, in St Andrews, the Queen Regent and Archbishop Hamilton sentenced Walter Myln, a harmless old priest in his eighty-third year, to be burnt at the stake. So shocked were the people of St Andrews that they would neither provide fuel nor bindings. The Provost himself refused to have anything to do with the dreadful business. But once more Patrick Hamilton and George Wishart had been forgotten and the Archbishop's servants carried out the sentence. The long summer days that year were loud with the riots provoked by this cruel and aimless sentence. When the new preachers were brought before the Queen-Regent to answer for their trouble-making they came with grim faced, heavily armed lairds to back them; men who declared their feelings about the bishops in strong words. 'They oppress us and our tenants to feed their idle bellies; they trouble our preachers and would murder them and us. Shall we suffer this any longer? No, Madam, we shall not!' Faced with these determined men, Mary of Guise thought it wiser simply to advise them to 'love their neighbour and go in peace.'

But there was to be little peace. On New Year's Day 1559, pinned to the doors of friars' houses and hospitals throughout the burghs of Scotland, there appeared, quite mysteriously, notices to quit. In the name of 'the blind, lame, bedridden, widows and orphans and all other poor,' they called upon the occupiers to get out and find honest work, leaving their riches to those in need. If they were still there on the 12th May, they would be thrown out with all necessary violence.

45

John Knox in Scotland

It was a call to war. New Church against Old. All that now remained was for a leader to come forth, behind whom the New Church could march. On the 2nd May at the port of Leith, John Knox returned to his native Scotland. He would be such a leader. The people of Scotland erupted in a great rage of senseless destruction. It began in Perth in St John's Church on Thursday, 11th May, the day before the friars were to quit their houses and riches. There John Knox preached and there a foolish boy threw a stone at a foolish priest who insisted on saying the Mass. The stone flew wide and smashed a holy image. The mob broke loose and smashed all the holy images in Perth and Scone; in St Andrews, Stirling and Linlithgow; and in Edinburgh and Holyrood. It was not what John Knox wanted, and not what the Lords of the Congregation planned. But the destruction was not as bad as it might have been. No blood was shed, no buildings destroyed.

A setback

In Scotland, the Queen-Regent waged war against the Protestant rebels from her strongly defended base in Leith. Her four thousand professional soldiers from France were more than a match for the forces of the New Church. A war with weapons was quite different from a war of words from the pulpit. By the wintry end of 1559 they had retreated from Edinburgh to Stirling, and from Stirling to Fife and Glasgow. The Frenchmen were now boldly striking into Fife and on the morning of 23rd January, 1560 were pushing north-east from Dysart across the River Leven. The strength of the New Church was crumbling before the Queen-Regent's French power and when more ships were sighted heading into the Firth of Forth it must have seemed that Scotland must now become Catholic and French.

Foreign aid

But the ships that sailed into the Firth flew not the French flag, but the Royal Standard of England. Commanded by Admiral Winter, the English Fleet

was coming to the aid of the Scots. The French supply line was cut and the Catholic army returned to Leith, where no reinforcements could enter whilst Winter's fleet guarded the Firth. In early April an English army crossed the border and together with the Scots Protestants laid siege to Leith. Mary of Guise died there on 11th June of a serious illness and peace was restored the following month by the Treaty of Edinburgh. By its terms the French were to withdraw, Elizabeth was seen to be the proper Queen of England and the Auld Alliance came to an end. The French soldiers were glad to go home, the English fleet was glad to take them and the Scots were glad to be left alone.

Reformation of the Church of Scotland

Parliament was summoned at Edinburgh in August 1560 and the Church of Scotland was officially reformed. The authority of the Pope was no longer recognised and Mass was forbidden. There was prepared a Confession of Faith which laid down the new Protestant beliefs. It was drawn up by ministers and approved by Parliament. Above all else it declared that the Bible was God's written word and the source of holy truth. The Reformation of the Church of Scotland had been carried through.

The Protestants succeeded in their struggle partly because of the energy and drive of John Knox and his fellow preachers and partly because continued friendship with France could offer little of value to Scotland. The new alliance with their old enemy in the south, sharing the same language and now the same religion, made greater sense and offered much more. The bitter wars that had raged between the two countries for nearly three centuries came to an end. Never again would Scotland be darkened under the shadow of English conquest.

Yet what had been won by the Reformation was less than Knox and others had wanted. Their vision of the New Church and what it meant was contained in an amazing document called the 'Book of Discipline', prepared in 1561 by John Knox and his fellow ministers. In it they planned a new structure, not only for the Church, but for the nation itself.

The feudal Catholic Church with overlords and common people, its rood screens and Latin services must give way to a kirk, where ministers are elected by the congregation they serve and are aided by elders drawn from that same congregation. There were to be no more bishops. Ten superintendents would look after the needs of a hundred parish ministers and their flocks. They would answer to the General Assembly of the Church of Scotland which, like Parliament, would be composed of men of rank, men of business and men of the Church.

Education

If congregations were to elect their own ministers then they must be well informed congregations. The nation must now be educated. For people of all classes the Church would provide an education service as ambitious as any ever devised. In every parish there would be primary and secondary schooling for all children. Grants of money would help the poorest. And there would be ample university training for those who could benefit from it, whatever their wealth or lack of it. The great cost of all this would be met out of the wealth of the Old Church.

The Book of Discipline was approved in part by the nobles and lairds, and the Church was reformed as planned. But the grander vision of service and education which would have been very costly was neglected. Funds that should have met the cost were taken instead by the nobles. Two thirds of the wealth of the Old Church stayed with those people who held it before. The remaining third was divided between Crown and Church, with the Crown taking an increasing share as the years passed. The grand design in the Book of Discipline which could have given the Scottish nation a full education service more than four centuries ago failed for want of cash. But the reformers had found their New Church.

(517)

THE
Firſt Book
OF
DISCIPLINE*.

To the great Councell of *Scotland* now admitted to the Regiment, by the Providence of God, and by the common Confent of the Eftates thereof, your Honours humble Servitors and Minifters of Chrift Jefus within the fame, wifh Grace, Mercy, and Peace from God the Father of our Lord Jefus Chrift, with the perpetuall Increafe of the holy Spirit.

FRom your Honours we received a Charge dated at Edinburgh the 29th of April, in the Yeare of our Lord 1560. requiring and commanding us in the Name of the eternall God, as we will anfwer in his Prefence, to commit to Writing, and in a Book deliver to your Wifedoms our Judgements touchiug the Reformation of Religion which heretofore in this Realme (as in others) hath been utterly corrupted; upon the Receit whereof (fo many of us as were in this Towne) Kk 3   did

* This Edition of the *Firft Book of Difcipline* is conformable to the Edition printed *Anno* 1621, the typographical Errors are corrected; fome Words which probably have been omitted by the Printer are fupplyed from other Copies, but they are printed in the *Saxon* Character; and a few various Readings are printed on the Foot-margin.

Worksection

A New Church
Understand Your Work

The Greenwich Agreement
1 Who was heir to the Scottish throne when James V died in 1542?
2 What relation was Henry VIII to the Scottish heir?
3 What marriage plan did Henry VIII have for his son?
4 Why did he want this marriage?
5 What was Henry's first step in making his plan work?
6 What demands did he make that caused his plan to fail?

The Church of Rome
1 What hardships did the common folk suffer in Scotland in the 16th Century?
2 What was it about the bishops and abbots that they objected to?
3 What did they feel about the parish priests?
4 How did they feel the church was behaving towards the poor and needy?
5 What were the payments often made for a funeral service?
6 What effect did the parish priests own poverty have on their behaviour?
7 What was wrong with the church services attended by the common folk?
8 What was a commendation and what was it for and why were they first introduced?
9 What did later kings use them for?
10 How did this damage the Church?

Protestants
1 What was upsetting people about their Church buildings in the middle of the 16th Century?
2 What did parliament think of how the Church was being run?
3 What other things about the Church were certain people protesting at?
4 What did these people believe was the most important thing about being a good Christian?
5 Who was the great leader of the Protestants in Europe?
6 How did the Scots learn about this preacher in Germany and what he was saying?
7 What advantages did the powerful men of the land see in the new religion?
8 What happened to the Treaty of Greenwich?

Henry attacks Edinburgh
1 How was Henry prevented from bribing Scotland's greedy nobles?
2 What did the English King do in his rage when his bribes failed?
3 How were the new Protestants thought of after Henry's savage attacks?
4 How did Cardinal Beaton try to stamp out the new religion?

5 What effect did this have?
6 What happened to Patrick Hamilton and George Wishart?
7 How was Cardinal Beaton encouraged to 'repent the shedding of Wishart's blood'?
8 What happened to Beaton's killers and their supporters?
9 Were they all treated with equal firmness?
10 What was John Knox's punishment?

Marriage demands
1 How did Protector Somerset continue Henry VIII's 'rough wooing' of Mary the Infant Queen?
2 What happened on Black Saturday?
3 How did Somerset use the English fleet during the battle and after it?
4 What did the Scots believe the English were trying to do?
5 Where did Scotland turn for aid?
6 What was demanded as the price for this help?

Mary of Guise
1 What was Mary of Guise, Queen-Regent, trying to do to Scotland?
2 How did she go about this?
3 What had happened in England that helped her?
4 What French plan was Mary of Guise playing her part in?
5 How successful was this new persecution of the Protestants?
6 Who were the 'Godlie Band'?
7 How did the people of St. Andrews feel about the execution of Walter Myln?
8 What happened on New Year's Day, 1559?

John Knox
1 What happened just ten days before the 'notices to quit' expired?
2 What effect did John Knox's preaching have on the people of Scotland?
3 Where and when did it all begin?
4 In what ways was the rioting not as bad as it might have been?
5 How did the Queen-Regent hit back?
6 From where did the Scottish Protestants get aid?

Reformation of the Church of Scotland
1 What happened in Parliament in August 1560?
2 What changes were made in the Church of Scotland?
3 How did Scotland now change its friendship with other countries?
4 Were John Knox and his followers now satisfied?
5 What was the 'Book of Discipline'?
6 What changes did it propose in the organisation of the church?

Education

1 Why was it thought important to have a new education system?
2 What schooling was to be provided?
3 How were the poor to be helped in their education?
4 Who was to be allowed to attend university?
5 Where was the money to come from?
6 Why was this grand scheme not put into practice?

Use Your Imagination

1 What do you think Henry VIII really wanted out of the wedding of his son to the Scottish Queen?

2 What do you think the common folk were thinking and saying about the rich bishops and abbots?

3 Do people say the same things today about certain members of society who seem to have more than their fair share of the good things?

4 How might you reform society today to help the poor in this country and in other countries?

5 Why did the people in the burghs begin to wonder if bishops were really necessary?

6 Do you think this struggle Scotland was having in the 16th century was *all* about religion?

7 Do ordinary folk today ever think that the services meant to help them do not receive enough support?

8 What do you think some people in the 16th century, who had wealth and power, thought about the idea of a new religion?

9 Do you think Henry VIII's methods for getting Scotland to agree to his wishes about the marriage of his son and the Scottish Queen were wise ones? How might he have done better? Why do you think he behaved the way he did?

10 What do you suppose people thought could happen to them after death, which could make them endure burning at the stake rather than change their religious beliefs?

11 What was the most important thing in a good Christian's life, according to the new Protestants?

12 Why do you think the axelike bill of the English soldiers was a better weapon than the long Scottish spear? When might it not be?

13 Why do you think England came to the aid of their old enemy, the Scots?

Further Work

1 The chapter called 'One Nation' in *A History of Scotland*, *Book 2*, describes events that followed the death of Alexander III. Read this section and see how it compares with 1542 and after.

2 Henry VIII wanted to hold the Scottish Castles because then he could control the country. Castles provide safe bases from which the garrisons can ride out and keep the people in order. To be safe a castle has to be built in a good position – not like this one!

Discuss this in your group and make a list of all the things you would look for in the ideal site for a castle.

3 Castles were more than strongholds – they were homes, not only for their owners but for all those who worked and served within them including the garrison. Copy this see-through diagram and plan the interior of your castle to provide places for – cooking, eating, sleeping, storing etc. (Just as you do at home).

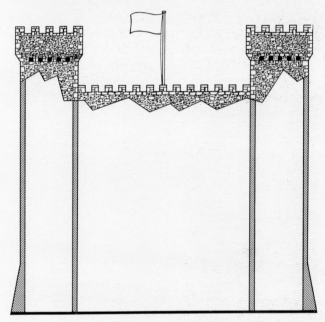

You can draw in this different rooms using a soft pencil. Start by drawing a thick line from side to side for each floor. There are usually two or three storeys and a basement.

Now add stairs leading from one floor to another. (These could be in the towers or in the main part).

Finally put in your rooms and show what each is for by drawing furniture, equipment etc, and adding the people, too. Coloured flags flying from the poles will brighten your picture.

4 Imagine you are an adviser to the Royal Court in England and write a report suggesting how the Scottish people might be persuaded that a marriage between Henry VIII's son Edward and Mary, Queen of Scots would be good for England. Can you think of times in the past when English kings have dealt with Scotland in the wrong way?

Queen of Scots

The Queen's return

Through the thick mist of the morning of 19th August, in the year 1561, there appeared in the Roads of Leith the ghostlike forms of two tall and stately craft. Only as they drew close, and separated from the sullen grey blanket that for two days hung over the Firth, could their dipping oars and limp standards be clearly seen. No one had known where to expect the ships. Away to the north-east at Aberdeen, the Earl of Huntly had made ready to receive them. But now, a week earlier than expected, the great vessels, one all white and the other red, flying the blue standard of France, eased gently towards Leith Harbour, the Port of Edinburgh. At about nine o'clock Mary, Queen of Scotland, returned to her homeland after thirteen years in France. She was not yet nineteen but already a widow. Her French husband, King Francis II, had died eight months before. She was Catholic and more French than Scots. There would be problems.

No longer Queen of France, Mary still had her kingdom in the north and she meant to govern it. She also had her ambitions in the south. Along with all Catholic Europe, she believed herself heir to the English throne. A Catholic heir to England's throne who was already Queen of a Catholic Scotland might easily prompt certain English Catholics to rid themselves of their present Queen, and speed Mary with her Church to their throne.

The quiet of her welcome was not only due to her surprise arrival. The chilliness had less to do with the drizzle and clinging mist than with the mood of the people. Their new reformed Church was a tender plant and John Knox feared that sorrow and darkness had entered the land with the Catholic Queen. He declared the days of thick mist that shrouded the city to be the frown of God. Mary herself could hardly have been overjoyed at her wet and fogbound realm. She who had been proclaimed Mary Queen of Scots, and of the French, and of the English and Irish now found herself with only the least of these.

A welcome

But people did cheer and cheer joyfully, when they actually saw their new Queen. She looked the part. Tall and beautiful, she carried herself with dignity and authority and though she was as French as any Frenchwoman, she could still speak in her native tongue. And while it may not have raised her spirits greatly, five or six hundred worthy Scots voices sang lusty psalms to the tuneless scraping of three-stringed fiddles beneath her window that night in Holyrood. It was a brave if not quite sincere welcome and, though she has been spared the bagpipes, the music itself was a far cry from what she had been used to in the soft luxury of the French royal court. But Mary thanked her entertainers and warmed their hearts by inviting them to continue on other evenings.

She had already upset her subjects by refusing to confirm the Treaty of Edinburgh which had ended the Reformation fighting. It would have meant agreeing that Elizabeth was the true Queen of England. She upset them again on the Sunday after her arrival when she made her way to the chapel royal at Holyrood. The news soon spread that she was hearing the forbidden Mass with her French companions. Riot flared and the mob all but broke into the chapel. At the very door itself they found the Lord James Stewart, Mary's Protestant half-brother and senior statesman. Not only had he given official permission for the private Mass, he had a healthy dislike of such wild and extreme behaviour. His resolute bearing cooled the violent anger and peace was restored.

A statue of John Knox

But it was never in Mary's mind to alter the new religion of her subjects. She publicly declared that she would not interfere, nor on pain of death would anyone else interfere, with the state of the Church or the beliefs of her people. She commanded a similar penalty for anyone who attacked her French servants in the practice of their religion. Mary planned to rule a Protestant Scotland, while remaining Catholic herself. She had other plans too.

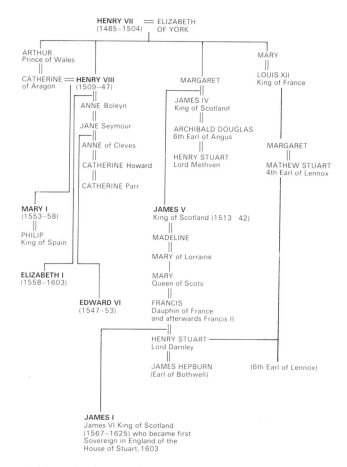

The House of Tudor

Ambitions in the south

It was towards the south that the young Queen looked longingly, knowing that her greatest ambition was to gain the throne of England. But first she must restore proper power to the Crown. She must be a real Queen of Scots, and this with no army, no wealth, no help from outside and few friends within. And with the particular distrust of Elizabeth, Queen of England, it was a steep road she had chosen.

Though Mary trod softly between her Protestant nation and her personal religion, she was not afraid to rebuke those who went too far in the name of their faith. John Knox himself was summoned to the palace more than once to answer for his wild preaching against the lawful queen. He was impressed by her quick mind and wisdom, if not her religious beliefs.

A tour of the realm

Less than a month after her arrival at Holyrood, the new queen set out on a tour of her realm. Wherever she went she was greeted by cheering crowds and special displays in her honour. They were usually very anti-Catholic the shows, and on one occasion it was actually planned, as part of Mary's entertainment, to burn the effigy of a priest, but it was thought to be in bad taste!

Her first visit was to her birthplace at Linlithgow, and then on to Stirling, Perth, Dundee, St Andrews, a brief stay at her father's favourite home at Falkland Palace and back to Holyrood, before September was out. What she saw on the tour left her in no doubt about two things: Her people were strongly for their new Church; she could win their loyalty if she continued to respect their faith. She wisely took as her chief adviser the Lord James Stewart, and appointed William Maitland of Lethington to be her Secretary of State. Both men were very able and both were Protestant, though not extreme in their beliefs. She saw to it also, that money was made available to the new Church from the third that had been awarded to the Crown. At home, Mary had started well.

Falkland Palace

Linlithgow Palace

The English Crown

England was another matter. Though Mary believed herself to be the rightful Queen of England she could hardly expect Elizabeth simply to step aside. Mary's best hope lay in persuading the English Queen to name her heir apparent to the English Crown. But Elizabeth was not at all keen on that plan. It seemed to her that she was being asked to arrange her own funeral. Mary would need to be very clever and very persuasive.

Within weeks of her return to Scotland Mary had dispatched William Maitland, to open the matter officially with Elizabeth. He set out that September and in London was granted an interview with the English Queen and her advisers. He offered the signing of the Treaty of Edinburgh in exchange for recognition of his Queen's claim.

Elizabeth admitted privately that she preferred Mary as her successor to any other but remained unwilling to make this public. She knew her subjects too well. They were 'more prone to worship the rising than the setting sun.' But she did agree to a change in the Treaty. Now Mary might sign it without giving away her right to be heir to the English throne after Elizabeth. And she also suggested that Secretary Maitland and her own William Cecil should continue privately to exchange letters on the subject.

Maitland's visit to London had been, by no means, a failure. For Mary the future looked bright. Her best plan now was to become more friendly with Elizabeth her cousin. But for this they must meet face to face. Mary's letters were affectionate, flattering and backed up with personal gifts – a diamond ring, a book of verse. Elizabeth responded warmly and, in time, the meeting to decide the destiny of the Crown of England was arranged to take place in Nottingham on 3rd September, 1562. Patience and Maitland's skill had brought Mary to the very point of success. On 6th July, Queen Elizabeth confirmed the arrangements, and two days later William Cecil drew up the royal safe conduct through the realm of England for Mary Queen of Scots.

William Maitland and Queen Elizabeth I
discuss the line of succession

The Huguenots

But, in Mary's beloved France, there had been trouble between Catholic and Protestant. It had begun some months before, on 1st March 1562. Mary's Catholic uncle, the Duke of Guise, had ordered his troops to fire on Huguenots at a prayer meeting in Vassy. Elizabeth of England now found herself due to travel to the north of her realm to meet Mary, a Catholic daughter of the house of Guise, while across the narrow English Channel French Protestants fought for their lives. She could not go. Instead Elizabeth signed a treaty of support for the Huguenots. On the 15th July the English Queen sent north her special envoy, Sir Henry Sidney, to inform her disappointed cousin that their meeting would not take place but that a new date should be arranged.

Portrait of Queen Elizabeth I

A trial of strength

It was in that same year that Mary was to face her first trial of strength in her own kingdom. In the middle of August 1562 she rode north on a royal tour of her highland realm. And she had a score to settle there. Some months before there had been a dispute over territory between Sir John Gordon, son of Huntly, and Lord John Ogilvie, a member of the royal household. In the skirmish that followed Sir John seriously wounded Lord Ogilvie and had been imprisoned. But then he escaped and returned unpunished to the safety of his father's earldom in the north. Mary would not let justice be so simply cheated.

While on her northern tour the Queen took a repentant Sir John prisoner. His repentance was brief. He escaped once more, and further angered his Queen by gathering a thousand wild horsemen to his banner. He had it in mind to sweep Mary on to his horse and take her for his wife. The Queen was not impressed.

On the 11th September Mary approached the castle at Inverness. She found it barred against her, on the orders of another son of the Earl of Huntly. But this was not a Huntly stronghold, it was a royal castle. When the Queen's party were finally admitted the garrison commander was hanged from the battlements for his treason.

In the simple square keep of Inverness, Mary took time to enjoy the autumn beauty of her northern realm. She was delighted to meet the hardy folk who dressed in skins and often slept amongst the heather. They came to see the beautiful girl whom they had been told was their queen. She dazzled her subjects in the silver and green of her highland dress. And her companions pleased them by wearing plaids. Mary Stuart (she spelled her name this way through error or French) was never happier than when in her savage and noble highlands. She flattered the young lairds, and the not so young, when she told how much she wished to be a man and share in their adventures.

Mary was as brave as any who rode with her. It was her own bright spirit that supported the less hardy of her train through the Huntly lands. The group was always shadowed by the menacing horsemen of Sir John Gordon; danger hung darkly at each corner, and over every woodland. From Inverness they made their way to Elgin and then nervously towards the crossing of the River Spey. Here the horsemen, lurking in the nearby tree cover, might easily strike. But no attack came and the royal party rode past the coastal stronghold of Castle Findlater on the Moray Firth, and south-east to a loyal and joyous welcome in Aberdeen on 22nd September.

But there was still the Catholic Earl of Huntly to deal with. The Queen could have no ruler but herself in the kingdom and she determined to bring Huntly to obedience or battle. He had gathered his forces on the eastern slopes of the Hill of Fare above the marshy hollow by the Corrichie Burn. On the 28th October, Mary's troops who had come the fifteen or so miles from Aberdeen, engaged the Gordons of Huntly in fierce fighting. The musket fire of the royal force drove the rebels down from their strong position and into the soft ground of the hollow where they fell easy prey to the Queen's men.

The Earl and two of his sons, Sir John and seventeen year old Adam, were taken prisoner during the battle. Huntly's weak heart gave way in the fighting and he fell dead from his horse. Sir John was executed for his treason within the week and in the presence of the young queen.

The executioner, perhaps too well fortified with ale or wine for the gruesome duty, bungled his work and Mary fainted. She was in a state of collapse for most of the next day and looked for no further revenge on the rebels of Corrichie. The Queen returned to Holyrood during November.

Plans for marriage

Her kingdom settled and at peace once more, Mary had time to turn again to her dreams of an English throne and of a royal husband to share her heavy burden as head of state. She looked abroad for princes who might fill Scotland's needs by bringing the friendship and support of their powerful states: Don Carlos of Spain, Archduke Charles of Austria, or even her brother-in-law, the young French King. And there were others too. But (in the eyes of Elizabeth of England) the children of great Catholic realms would not make for Mary a wise choice of husband. She made that clear enough. What she did not make half so clear was the choice that would please her. Mary was anxious to know from her cousin the names of suitable bridegrooms, not a list of the unsuitable ones. Elizabeth hinted that the Earl of Leicester might be a proper choice but he was the man most likely to marry Elizabeth herself. Maitland could not take this suggestion seriously and replied lightly that it would be better if Elizabeth married Leicester and made Mary heir to both her crown and Leicester!

Henry Darnley

In the end fate took a hand. It was not because Mary believed it would please Elizabeth, though she may have thought it would. It was not because the Earl of Moray (Lord James) or William Maitland advised it. They did not. And it was certainly not because she had secured her claim to the Crown of England. This was as far away as ever. It was simply because she had fallen hopelessly and helplessly in love that, on Sunday 29th July, 1565, in the Chapel Royal at Holyrood and by a Catholic service, a radiantly happy Mary was joined in marriage with Henry Darnley who was proclaimed King Henry of Scotland by the royal heralds.

At once there was trouble. Her once loyal and trusted half brother, Moray, who had enjoyed his position as adviser and 'shadow king', objected most strongly to the young, conceited and foolish Darnley. In August, shortly after the royal wedding, rebel troops gathered to Moray's banner at the Royal Burgh of Ayr. Mary responded at once by ordering her host to muster at Edinburgh on the 22nd August. Four days later she rode out through the city gates to lead her loyal army, herself steel helmeted and with a pistol by her side. Her escort, Lord Darnley, now King Henry, for all the splendour of his gilt armour, was outshone by Mary's sparkling spirit. As the Queen's men rode westwards towards Ayr, Moray led his troops towards Edinburgh, and entered the Capital on the last day of the month. There he had a chilly

reception from a people who had come to admire and trust their young queen. Under the sullen threat of the Castle Guns and with Mary now at Glasgow to meet her men from the north, the rebels thought again and made quickly for Dumfries. Chased by an angry Queen, the Earl of Moray fled across the border to the safety of England. The rebels were thoroughly put down in what came to be known as the Chase-About Raid.

Now Mary ruled supreme. All power was hers. Now too, she discovered to her sorrow how useless was the creature she had married. Deeply disappointed she made sure that her vain, spineless, spiteful husband would have no royal power. She turned to others for help, in particular David Riccio. In Mary's eyes he was 'a trusty servant' but to John Knox and to the Protestant Lords he was 'a vile knave', another Catholic to threaten the new Church. To Darnley he was a rival for his wife's affection and this filled the proud, headstrong King with blind rage.

Portrait of Lord Darnley and his younger brother

Murder of Riccio

On the evening of 9th March 1566, Mary was at supper in her private apartments in Holyrood with David Riccio and a few other friends. Though it was Lent, the Catholic Queen was having meat served because she was now expecting a child. Suddenly the figure of Darnley appeared in the doorway. Then behind him, and more alarmingly, a ghostlike creature in steel cap and armour, his eyes burning against the sickly white of his skin. The glaring figure was Patrick, Earl of Ruthven who had risen from his sick bed. Why they had come was soon enough clear when Ruthven gruffly demanded that Riccio should come out of the chamber. 'Let it please your Majesty that yonder man David come forth from your privy-chamber where he has been over long.' Neither the Queen's command nor her pleading could stay the fevered Ruthven and his wild followers, and Darnley looked on as Riccio was dragged from the chamber, his clinging fingers wrenched from Mary's skirts. Begging desperately for her aid, and justice, David Riccio was hacked to death under more than fifty dagger strokes.

The following morning the empty, swaggering Darnley was back in Holyrood. He took Mary's seeming forgiveness as proof of her belief that he had played no part in the murder. But Mary had wept already for her friend and adviser in secret sorrow and anger. Now her tears were dry and she thought more upon revenge.

Two nights later in the early hours of Tuesday 12th March, Mary and Darnley stole quietly from Holyrood, down the stairs the murderers had used, and out through a kitchen door to waiting horses and a small loyal escort. Under cover of dark they cleared the sleeping capital and rode at speed for Dunbar until the black shapes of approaching horsemen loomed suddenly in their path. Whatever panic seized the fleeing couple was quietened when the mounted troop wheeled to form an escort about the royal party and rode with them to the castle of James Hepburn, Earl of Bothwell. There, within the safety of its stout stone walls and after five hard hours ride, the Queen cooked a breakfast of eggs for the loyal men who had aided her rescue.

Within a week, Mary Queen of Scots rode once more into Edinburgh at the head of eight thousand men. The murderers of Riccio made a wise and hurried journey south to England where they would be safe. They would not forget how Darnley had betrayed them.

Birth of an heir

On the 19th June 1566, with the kingdom at rest, the great guns of Edinburgh Castle boomed out over a capital bright with bonfires, to salute the birth of Mary's son James. The child did nothing to bring Mary and her husband closer. In the Autumn of that year Mary was wondering if divorce would free her from unhappy marriage but feared that James would lose his right to the throne, not only of Scotland but of England too. Darnley did not attend his son's christening on the 17th December that year and by Christmas Mary had pardoned Riccio's killers. They returned to Scotland in January 1567, revenge in their hearts.

The Lord Darnley, King of Scotland in name only, had few friends now and had been gravely ill with smallpox since Christmas. At Mary's request he was brought from Glasgow to Edinburgh at the end of January so that she might nurse him to recovery at Kirk o' Field, a pleasant house just within the city wall. She visited him several times and stayed at the house on Wednesday and Thursday the 5th and 6th of February. And on the Sunday she came again, from a ball with some of her earls, all in their splendid carnival costumes. As the evening wore on the visitors withdrew leaving Darnley and his valet alone in the house.

Later that night the house transformed itself, with a shattering roar, into a great red and yellow plume of fire and smoke. The bodies of Lord Darnley, King of Scotland and his valet were found in the garden. To this day nobody is sure how they died. Some say that they were killed in the explosion, others say that they were choked to death, whilst trying to escape. When Darnley died he was only twenty-one years of age.

Though several men were later punished for the part they played in it no one was ever brought properly to justice for the murder of Henry Darnley and his manservant. It was believed by many that the Queen's friend, James Hepburn, Earl of Bothwell bore the most guilt. A trial of sorts did take place in Edinburgh but the with the capital filled with Bothwell's men no one thought it wise to support the charges against him. He was acquitted. He even threatened to fight any man who would still call him guilty and, under armed persuasion, almost thirty nobles signed a statement of Bothwell's innocence. They also declared that he would be a proper replacement for the murdered King Henry.

After the explosion at Kirk o'Field

The Earl of Bothwell

This was the man that, on 15th May 1567, in the great hall of Holyrood, Mary Queen of Scots took as her husband. With that ceremony the shadows finally closed over Mary Stuart's life.

This hasty marriage, only three months after the brutal murder at Kirk o' Field, shocked the people deeply. That the guilty man should now be the Queen's husband was beyond their endurance. Out of their anger grew rebellion. What little support Mary and Bothwell could muster was overcome without battle. Outlawed and unable to help himself or the Queen further, Bothwell fled the country. He went first to Orkney and Shetland and then to Denmark, where he died in madness, shackled to a dungeon wall.

Mary herself had surrendered on 15th June, 1567, to her Protestant lords. When the captive Queen was brought to Edinburgh the good people, who had recently cheered her, now called for her to be burnt at the stake. Instead, and with no more justice, she was imprisoned in the stern fastness of Loch Leven's lonely island castle in Kinross. On the 24th July she was forced to abdicate. Within the week her year old son was crowned James VI, King of Scotland. Within the month her half-brother, the Earl of Moray was appointed regent.

The death of Bothwell

Exile in England

But Mary was not yet finished. She escaped from her prison in the May of 1568 and at once raised an army. At Langside near Glasgow the Queen's troops were defeated by Moray, and Mary fled the field. She rode south with sixteen companions, to cross the border at Solway and throw herself on her royal cousin's mercy. In the bleak years that followed, Mary was moved from one castle prison to another where she was ever more carefully watched. Never was she allowed to meet the English Queen. Always there were the Catholic plots, real and invented, which formed around her. Always she was seen as a threat to Elizabeth's life. At last, after almost twenty miserable years, she was brought to the grim castle of Fotheringhay. There on the winter morning of 8th February, 1587, she entered the great hall. Tall and gracious, Mary walked with dignity and in silence to mount the three steps to the black-draped platform. She prayed for some time and then, her black robe removed, she knelt, all in red, before the block. She died not for reasons of justice but because it suited the purposes of the English Crown (which she had so longed to wear) to have brave Mary Stuart, sometimes Queen of Scots, silenced by the executioner's axe.

Queen of Scots
Understand Your Work

The Queen's return
1 Did Mary arrive when she was expected?
2 Apart from Leith, where else was it thought the Queen would arrive?
3 How long had she been a widow?
4 Why were there likely to be problems for Mary?
5 Where did her real ambition lie?
6 Who was particularly upset at the idea of a Catholic Queen on the Scottish throne?
7 How do you think Mary felt about her new kingdom?

A Welcome
1 What caused the people to be pleased about their new Queen?
2 How did they make her welcome?
3 What type of instrument accompanied the psalms?
4 Why did Mary not sign the treaty of Edinburgh?
5 What did Mary do on the Sunday after she arrived which upset her subjects?
6 Were they right to think she planned to change their Church?
7 What special difficulties had Mary in making herself a real Queen of Scotland?
8 How did she deal with John Knox?

The English Crown
1 What was it that Mary wanted Elizabeth of England to agree to?
2 Did Elizabeth believe Mary was entitled to this?
3 What was Elizabeth unwilling to admit in public and why?
4 What did Elizabeth agree to, that was of help to Mary?
5 Who were Mary's main advisers?
6 How did Mary think she could improve her chances of succeeding Elizabeth?
7 How did she try to arrange this?
8 What happened in another country which made this impossible?

A Trial of Strength
1 Why had Sir John Gordon been imprisoned?
2 What did he do after his second escape?
3 What was Sir John's ambition?
4 How did Mary feel about her Highland subjects?
5 What particularly pleased them about her?
6 Why was Mary's surname spelt 'Stuart' and not like her father's 'Stewart'?
7 How safe did the royal party feel on this Highland tour?
8 Why did Mary bring the Earl of Huntly to battle at Corrichie Burn?
9 What happened to Sir John Gordon?
10 How did Mary react to this?

Plans for marriage
1 Who were the people Mary considered as possible husbands?
2 In what way did Elizabeth fail to advise Mary?
3 Why, in the end, did Mary choose Henry Darnley?
4 Was it a good choice?
5 What did Lord James Stewart do after this marriage?
6 What was the Chase-About Raid?
7 What did Mary discover about her husband and what did she do about it?
8 How did Darnley regard David Riccio?

Murder of Riccio
1 Where was David Riccio murdered?
2 Why was the Catholic Queen having meat during lent?
3 What was the first warning that something bad was going to happen that night?
4 How was Riccio killed?
5 Who led his murderers?
6 Why did Darnley think Mary believed him to be innocent?
7 Who helped Mary after her escape from Holyrood?
8 How did Mary take back control?

Birth of an heir
1 When was Mary's son James born?
2 Why did Mary not want to escape from her unhappy marriage by divorce?
3 How did Riccio's killers feel about Lord Darnley?
4 Where was Darnley lodged in Edinburgh?
5 How was he murdered?
6 Was justice done to the murderers?
7 Who was thought to be their ring-leader?
8 How did he make sure that he was found not guilty of the murder?

The Earl of Bothwell
1 When did Mary marry Bothwell?
2 Why were the people so shocked by this marriage?
3 What happened as a result of the people's anger?
4 How did Mary's son James become King?
5 Where was the battle at which Mary was defeated?
6 Why was she sentenced to death?
7 Where and when was Mary, Queen of Scots executed?

Use Your Imagination

1 The Earl of Huntly was the chief noble in the Catholic north-east of Scotland. Why do you think he expected Mary to land at Aberdeen instead of Leith?

2 What do you suppose John Knox meant when he described the thick mist that hung over Edinburgh at the time of Mary's arrival as the 'frown of God'?

3 Imagine you are Mary arriving in Scotland on a chilly wet and misty day after living in luxury and warmth in France. Write down some of the thoughts you might have on your first glimpse of your new kingdom where you are now to live and rule.

4 What feelings might Mary have had when six hundred Scottish musicians turned up to play and sing beneath her window? What might she have thought about the welcome – the music?

5 What do you think is meant by the statement that 'Mary trod softly between her Protestant nation and her personal religion?

6 In what ways do you think Mary began her reign well? Could her respect for the new religion upset anyone within Scotland? Could it upset people in other countries?

7 Do you think if Mary and Elizabeth had met as planned in September 1562, Mary would have been named as the heir to the English throne?

8 Throughout her tour of the Highlands, Mary was in constant danger of attack and had to fight a battle. Do you think there is anything surprising about the fact that she seemed to be in more danger there than in the Lowlands, with John Knox and his followers?

9 What made it so difficult for Mary to find a husband that would please everyone she wanted to please?

10 Why do you think Mary pretended to believe that Darnley played no part in the murder of David Riccio?

11 You are riding with Mary to Dunbar on her escape from Holyrood. Suddenly armed horsemen loom up out of the dark to surround you. Write a description of your thoughts at that moment. Finish off with the relief you feel when you discover they are friendly.

12 How do you suppose Darnley felt when he heard that the murderers of Riccio had been pardoned and were returning to Scotland?

13 What do you suppose was the main reason that Mary was finally executed?

Further Work

1 Here is a method by which you can make a picture of the French galleys appearing out of the mist in the Roads of Leith to bring Mary, Queen of Scots home to her kingdom. It is called a monoprint because only one print may be made from each original. You will need chalky crayons, sugar paper, newsprint and a sponge.

A Cover the sugar paper with a pale grey seascape of swirling mist using the chalks this way on their sides.

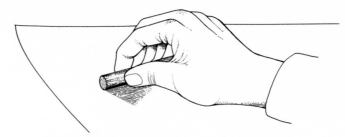

Put the sheet safely aside.

B Now draw the two galleys on separate sheets of newsprint, their sails hanging limp, their flags drooping as the oars dip and sweep in the still water. Use your chalks thickly.

C Now place one galley face down on the sea and thoroughly wet the back with your sponge. Press firmly with a wad of dry paper to make the monoprint and carefully peel off the newsprint to leave a faint misty print.
Repeat with your other galley.

You may need to experiment a number of times with this method to get the result you want.

When you are satisfied mount your picture for display to the rest of the class.

2 Imagine you were on the quayside at Leith when out of the grey mist loomed the two ghostlike forms of the French galleys. The Queen had come at last. Write a description of her arrival, of her appearance. Say how you felt, how the crowd behaved. The illustration on page 50 will help you.

3 Trace on a map Mary's tour of her kingdom which is described on page 52. How many miles did she cover in about a fortnight by horseback on Scotland's very rough roads?

4 Mary wrote letters to Elizabeth to flatter her and show that she was no threat to the English Queen. She was trying to arrange a meeting. See if you can write such a letter – just as though you were Mary.

5 If possible try to visit Holyrood Palace in Edinburgh where you will see the rooms used by Mary and also the scene of Riccio's murder.

6 In your group prepare a short play called 'The Death of David Riccio', and act it out for the rest of the class. It will make your play much better if you use the library to learn more about the events of that night. For example, here is what Mary herself said of the murder – '. . . Lord Ruthven entered demanding to speak to Riccio, and we asked if the King, our husband, knew anything of this, but he denied it. We also said that Riccio would go before the Lords in Parliament, if anyone wished to punish him. But Lord Ruthven and his accomplices advanced on Riccio who had gone behind my back, and they laid violent hands on him – some struck him over the shoulders and others stood in front of me with pistols, and at the door of my room they stabbed him fifty-six times with swords and daggers, at which I was in great fear for my life . . .'

61

United Kingdom

On 22nd January 1570, in the unlit upper room of a house in Linlithgow, belonging to the Archbishop of St Andrews, a man called James Hamilton worked quietly and carefully. He had laid a soft mattress on the floor to muffle any sounds he might make. At the window over the front stair he arranged the drapes so that he could see without being seen. He bolted the front door securely to prevent a hurried entry there. Now he only had to wait.

On the following day the Earl of Moray, Regent of Scotland since 1567 when Mary's crown was placed on her infant son's head, rode through Linlithgow, threading his way slowly among the packed crowds. He was shot dead.

Key towns and cities in Scotland of the sixteenth century

The Hamilton's bid for power

Hamilton escaped from his secret room through the back of the house and on a fast horse to the safety of Hamilton Palace. Scotland was without proper leadership yet again. It was the usual struggle amongst power-hungry nobles, only now there were Protestants to fight Catholics, King's men to fight Queen's men. For the nobles these ideas mattered less than their private wars. The 'Good Regent' died because the Hamiltons, led by the aging Earl of Arran, now returned from his rich dukedom in France, yearned for political power. They, along with most of the nobles, supported Mary, if they supported anything other than themselves.

In the next eight years, while Mary fretted in her English prison, Scotland went through three regents. Only the last of these survived much over a year. First came the Earl of Lennox, Lord Darnley's father. He was not popular but was the choice of Elizabeth of England. To support him she sent a small army which destroyed the Palace and Town of Hamilton. It was better revenge than strategy, for Mary's men still held Edinburgh Castle. Now Scotland had two parliaments. One was loyal to Lennox and the King's men in Stirling. The other in Edinburgh supported Mary. Each met in order to call threats and names at the other. But Lennox had the five year old King, and a new crown to replace the one still in Edinburgh.

Whoever held the King held the power.

Some of Mary's 'loyal' nobles, seeing this, changed sides. Others, Arran's Hamiltons and the Gordons of Huntly, made different plans. On the evening of 3rd September 1571, four hundred night riders left Edinburgh and rode towards Stirling. They made swift and quiet passage through the sleeping town and seized the Regent and as many of the King's earls as they could carry.

But they did not get far. Out through its gates and down into the town rode the garrison behind their commander, the Earl of Mar. Together with the armed townsmen they drove off the kidnappers, empty handed, amid the spatter of musketfire. But a parting gunshot, fired in panic or spite, mortally wounded Regent Lennox in the back. It was the Earl of Mar who became Regent after the death of Lennox. He made an unsuccessful attempt to recover Edinburgh Castle and after some months of bitter civil war, this peace-loving man died, broken in heart and spirit.

The man behind the raid was Sir James Kirkcaldy of Grange, garrison commander at Edinburgh Castle and Scotland's foremost soldier, but he had planned a swift and silent kidnapping, not looting and murder. In anger and disappointment he called the bungling leaders of the raid 'disorderly beasts', for the fatal shot must prove no less deadly to their cause than it had to Regent Lennox. There was no hope now of bargaining with the King's men and little chance of victory.

Portrait of Mary Queen of Scots

Portrait of the Earl of Mar

A Douglas

Now, and for the last time, a strong Douglas would lead Scotland. James Douglas, Earl of Morton, lead the King's party when Mar died in October 1572, and in November he became Regent. New hope was growing in the hearts of the Queen's men. News had reached them of the massacre of French Protestants on St Bartholemew's Eve. Surely a more determined Catholic France would come to the aid of Sir James Kirkcaldy in Edinburgh Castle, surrounded by the Earl of Morton's soldiers.

On the same day, 24th November, that Morton was elected Regent, John Knox died. He was buried in the churchyard of St Giles. He had fought a life-long battle for his new faith, preaching a gospel that sometimes sounded closer to hate than love, made more of fear than comfort. But he had defended a tender young Church against powerful men who sought to crush it for personal greed. In death he was remembered at his graveside by the new Regent, as 'one who neither feared nor flattered any flesh.'

The Massacre of St Bartholemew's Eve did bring aid to Scotland. In April 1573 ships arrived at Leith carrying great cannons, and an army led by Sir William Drury. But the help was not from France. Elizabeth of England was lending her support, and it was not for the Queen's men but for Morton. With great English siege guns to batter down the walls, and hardened English soldiers in trenches dug in Edinburgh's High Street, the castle could not stand for long. On 28th May, after eleven days bombardment, it fell. Sir James Kirkcaldy, its commander, thought by the King of France and many others, to be 'one of the most valiant men of our time', was hanged. The struggle was over.

The Earl of Morton governed firmly and well, but in 1580 he was brought to trial for the part he had played in Darnley's murder. A year later he went to the block, still protesting his innocence.

The massacre of St. Bartholemew's Eve

James's education

James VI turned fifteen in the month of Morton's execution. He had already received a deep and thorough education from his senior tutor George Buchanan, a terrifying man of stern and towering mind. Hour by hour, for ten long years at Stirling Castle, the boy king had learned eagerly. But his tutor had taught him more than Latin and Greek, French and Scots, History and Politics; more even than the Protestant Faith. He taught that kings ruled only by the consent of the people. He even taught that the people had a duty to kill a bad king. It was what John Knox had preached. There was little love or comfort in the young King's life, only discipline and punishment, and always the message that his mother Mary, still Elizabeth's captive, was an enemy to be hated. Buchanan even rewrote the history books to prove it.

But James would not believe all that his harsh old tutor told him. Among the six hundred books of his personal library, he found ideas better to his liking. He preferred to think that God and kings enjoyed a special relationship and that both were set high above the people and their Church; not at all what Knox had preached. George Buchanan had perhaps warped more than shaped his pupil. His carefully taught hatred of Mary twisted the young King's thinking. When Elizabeth of England had his mother executed in 1587 he hardly protested. But it was clear that James had inherited all Mary's craving for the English crown. He realized, however, that there could be no profit in a vengeful war with the south.

Anne of Denmark

It was late in the autumn of 1589 when James, now twenty-three, set out across a cold and restless North Sea to fetch home his royal bride, the Princess Anne of Denmark. He spent the winter in the Danish Court celebrating his wedding in hospitable Viking manner. The royal couple arrived in Scotland on May Day 1590 and James soon learned that not everyone wished him well on this happy return.

James VI as a boy

Portrait of Anne of Denmark

Witchcraft

Crazed old women now on trial in North Berwick were confessing to crimes of witchcraft, and not just ordinary black magic at that. Behind them was another Bothwell, nephew to Mary's husband. He was their warlock. At his command they had summoned great storms at sea as the King sailed home, and they cast deadly spells over his image in wax. But it was the witches who were to die, and in great numbers for years to come. The King was so terrified that he felt his whole kingdom to be in mortal peril from the power of the black arts. He wrote a book called *Demons* explaining how they exercised their evil influence. All over Scotland demented old women, found guilty of witchcraft, were burnt at the stake for the good of their souls. It was sad for the nation that their best educated king should become its most superstitious. Yet James had real enough reasons to

fear Bothwell. The Earl was on the verge of madness. More than once he had attacked James in Holyrood, hammering on doors and waving his naked sword before his king, even attempting to kidnap him.

Population

The land to which James had brought his royal bride was still a nation mainly of countrymen. Less than one fifth of the whole population, now about 700,000, lived in the busy burghs. Most people stayed where the soil was rich: towards the mouth of the Tweed and on the shores of the Solway; in Moray and on the banks of the Forth and Clyde. As many people lived north of the Tay as to the south of it, and with quietness restored to the kingdom men could reap what they had sown without English soldiers or retreating defenders to scorch the good earth.

A witch's bridle, one of the many punishments devised for 'witches'

Title page of James VI's book on 'demons', published 1597, in Edinburgh

James VI and Anne of Denmark

James VI interrogating witches, from a contemporary engraving

The Highlands

The Highlanders spoke Gaelic and were closer to the Celt than were the Lowland Scots, who by now thought themselves to be Anglo-Saxon. They cast fearful glances at the gloomy hills from whose shadows would plunge 'wyld and wykhed helandmen' to sweep away their cattle and burn their houses.

Such raiding would seem reasonable enough to a Celt who believed that the land belonged, not to kings and lords, but to the people. They were merely sharing by force what should be theirs by right – some of the produce of the richer, more fertile south. And they raided one another too, which made the problems of farming scanty soil even more difficult.

Nor were the Highlanders a feudal people. Their loyalties were to kinfolk. The clans were extended families, some large enough for a chief to command more than three thousand fighting men armed with longbow and musket, Lochaber axe, sword and dirk, and with a round studded shield for protection.

Like all Scots the Highlander's living came from the soil; and wherever it was good enough, clusters of low farm houses were gathered. There were seldom more than a dozen or fewer than six. The land was tilled with a light horse-drawn plough, four to a team, with three men to guide it. Ground too awkward for the plough was turned by càs chrom, a kind of plough spade.

In their rainswept glens they raised what crops they could. They preferred their long-haired cattle to sheep. At the day's end they sheltered in their squat, dark houses, turf-walled with the roof borne on a frame of timber cruks that rose within the thickness of the walls and bent at the eaves to meet at the ridge. Their peat fire burned smokily in the centre hearth and the floor was of hard-packed clay.

The chiefs had better dwellings, usually two storied and of stone; sometimes square keeps or even grander castles from which they could resist invaders, including the King, if necessary. There also, in the great hall, they feasted and were entertained by piper and harpist, minstrel and bard.

The Celtic Gael enjoyed singing, dancing and telling stories through the light, soft evenings spent at the summer grazings. They hunted with their chief and competed in running and throwing which were their Highland Games.

Transport

What roads there were in Scotland had no better surface than the tramped earth: a scanty network of tracks between castles and burghs. Travel throughout the kingdom was best on horseback. Goods went fastest by waterway. Trains of pack-horses plodded over the higher slopes above marsh and risk of ambush, but they carried only small items. It was easier to import timber from Norway than it was to bring it overland from the great forests of the Highland Glens.

Burghs

And still through plague and war the burghs prospered. More of the houses were stone-built now and some windows were glazed. The hard-headed, hard-striving merchant burgess now enjoyed the luxury of rooms panelled in wood with ceiling boards brightly painted and patterned. Furniture was thinly spread but solid, and bed chamber walls were softened with hanging tapestries. On the bare flooring stood a curtained bed and, under a cherished mirror, the table with horn-comb and soap and other items for personal grooming. There would be his wife's spinning wheel too. Elsewhere, and proudly displayed, were the burgess's necessary weapons: a long Scots spear and a two handed broadsword, a steel cap and a heavy leather jerkin. In his brown doublet and red hose, the Scottish burgess was the proud lord of his own household. While life was cruder than in most European countries, it was comfortable enough.

Beyond the heavy studded front door and down the forestair little had changed. But there was now *more* of everything – more people, more religion, more rubbish, more filth, more smell. And there was more trade too. On the harbour side gangs of men toiled, loading the square-rigged merchantmen that crowded into the burgh ports. There were bales of wool, and of linen and woollen cloth; of skins and hides; there were knitted stockings, gloves and bonnets. Up the gang planks the dockers rolled barrels of salt-herring and salmon, beef and butter, and sometimes honey and beer. They also herded cattle and other livestock over these narrow boards. Cartloads of coal, lead ore and salt were heaved on board. When fully laden the ships eased out through the narrow harbour mouths and, before straining sails, made way for France, the Netherlands, Poland and Scandinavia, and for Ireland and England too.

And they brought cargoes *into* the burgh ports. Bars of iron from Sweden and Spain; timber planks, spars and barrel staves from Norway; flax and hemp, tar and pitch, iron and copper from Poland and, in lean years corn too; half a million gallons of wine from France and Spain, with prunes and walnuts; spices from the Netherlands and clothing too, of silk and fur; dolls, rattles and chess sets; paper, parchment and harp strings; swords, guns and armour, thimbles and tobacco and much, much more.

The New Church armed with a *Second Book of Discipline* enforced quieter Feast Days and Sundays. The country was now divided in six hundred parishes, each with its elected kirk session to watch over the congregation. Those who broke the Sabbath by working or selling, playing, dancing or singing would be called upon to repent and fined. In more serious cases, and for the saving of souls, punishments of disgrace, pain and even death by burning could be ordered. The stocks and the scourge, the ducking-stool and stake all brought people to repentance in the name of Christ.

The Church

Out of a need for wiser ministers, and a wiser congregation, the New Church pressed forward with its plans for schooling. There were more grammar schools in the burghs and, in 1582, a fourth university, at Edinburgh joined the others which were being greatly expanded. Education was not free, but nobody was banned simply because of poverty. Those who could pay did so, and those who could not were granted aid.

Out of fear for the life of their new faith, and hatred of the Old Church, little had been done to restore the lovely abbeys and cathedrals. They lay in decay, their slender windows of multi-coloured glass shattered, their beautifully carved screens and choirs smashed and burned by the waves of English invasion. But now repair work was beginning, at Dunfermline, Melrose, Holyrood, at Aberdeen and in Leith; in cathedrals all over the country. And there were new churches too though they did not soar skywards like David I's wondrous abbeys. These were more modest buildings, usually long and with little decoration, poorly lit and heated.

Building

The King played his part in the new building with additions to his palaces of Linlithgow and Dunfermline and at Edinburgh Castle. But the best of it was neither royal nor holy. There was Earl Patrick Stewart's beautiful Palace of Kirkwall in Orkney with its pulpit windows and corbelled turrets. There was the glorious inner wall of Crichton Castle quilted, Italian-style, in low pyramids of cut and polished stone. And the most graceful of all Scotland's tower houses was William Forbes's lovely Craigievar, with its marvellous roof-top pinnacles and richly moulded plaster ceilings.

Craigievar Castle, Aberdeenshire

New ideas

In Scotland it was a time of invention and creation in science, art, commerce and industry. In the square tower house of Merchiston Castle in Edinburgh, John Napier, scientist and mathematician, took time off designing possible submarines and tanks, to invent what we know today as logarithms. Further north at Culross, Sir George Bruce mined coal from under the sea. Even further north in Sutherland, Jean Gordon, Bothwell's wife before Mary, had set up a coal mine and salt pans at Brora. (Coal is still privately mined there today.) Men laboured underground to dig out sixty thousand tons of coal a year from Scotland's soil, much of it to be exported. A deep water harbour was being built at Cockenzie and a breakwater planned for Stonehaven. The whole land was alive with a restless spirit and new dreams filled the minds of men.

Good news for James

This was the kingdom that James ruled, and ruled more strongly than any king before him. It was a nation at peace and making progress. It was a nation of much poverty and some wealth. Into its capital on the evening of Saturday 27th March, 1603, rode Sir Robert Carey with the word that Elizabeth of England was dead. On the last day of the month a second messenger brought the long awaited news that James VI of Scotland was now James I of England.

Worksection

United Kingdom
Understand your work

The Hamiltons' bid for power
1 What was James Hamilton preparing to do in Linlithgow on 22nd January 1570?
2 How did he escape?
3 What was the result of Hamilton's actions?
4 Who chose the Earl of Lennox to be Regent of Scotland while Mary was a prisoner in England?
5 What gave Lennox an advantage over those who were still loyal to Mary?
6 How did some of Mary's men try to alter this?
7 What did Sir James Kirkcaldy think of the way the raid on Stirling was carried out?
8 What effect had the killing of Lennox on the hopes of Mary's supporters?

A Douglas
1 From whom did James Douglas, Earl of Morton, take over the regency?
2 What had encouraged the supporters of Mary to think they would get French help?
3 Who died on 24th November 1572 and where is he buried?
4 From where did help come and from whom?
5 What happened to Sir James Kirkcaldy?
6 Which of the three regents proved to be the most able?
7 What was his fate?

James VI
1 Who educated James VI in his early years?
2 What subjects did he study at Stirling Castle?
3 What extra message did his tutor try to teach him?
4 How was James made to feel about his mother, Mary, Queen of Scots?
5 What was James not prepared to believe?
6 What did he prefer to think?
7 How did James behave when Elizabeth of England had his mother executed?
8 When was James married and to whom?

Witchcraft
1 Who were on trial in North Berwick when James returned from Denmark with his bride in 1590?
2 Who was their leader and what were they accused of?
3 How did James react to witchcraft?
4 What was happening throughout the country?
5 What real reason had James for fearing Bothwell (nephew of Mary's husband)?
6 How many people lived in Scotland's burghs in James's reign?
7 Where did the bulk of the population live?
8 Why was it now possible to farm more successfully than before?

The Highlands
1 In what ways did the Highlanders differ from the Lowland Scots?
2 What did the Lowlanders feel about the Highlandmen?
3 Why did the Highlanders think it reasonable to be raiders?
4 What was a clan?
5 What weapons did the fighting men use?
6 How did the Highland folk find their living?
7 How were the chiefs entertained?
8 What has happened now to the sports they enjoyed in the Highlands in James's time?

Transport
1 What condition were the roads of James's Scotland kept in?
2 What places did they link?
3 What was the best way to travel on the roads?
4 By what means were goods transported overland?
5 What were the quickest routes for carrying heavy goods?

Burghs
1 How were the houses constructed in James's burghs?
2 What kind of interior decoration did they have?
3 What weapons were burgesses required to keep?
4 Describe the conditions in the streets of the burghs?
5 What type of shops crowded the burgh harbour?
6 What goods were exported through these ports?
7 What was imported?
8 On what days did the bustle of the busy burgh cease?

The Church
1 How was the keeping of the Sabbath enforced?
2 Why was education now given to more people?
3 In what way were poor people helped to take part in the education system?
4 What repair work was now taking place in the churches of Scotland?
5 What type of design was used for new church buildings?
6 Where were the finest examples of building to be found at this time in Scotland?

New Ideas
1 What scientist worked on Merchiston Castle in Edinburgh?
2 What kinds of work was he engaged in?
3 What was unusual about Sir George Bruce's coal mine at Culross?
4 Where else was coal being mined and salt extracted from sea water?
5 How much coal was produced in Scotland in a year?
6 What other major works were taking place at this time in Scotland?
7 On Wednesday 31st March, 1603, a special proclamation was made. What was it?

Use Your Imagination

1 Why do you think James Hamilton was worried about the noise his movements might make on the floor?

2 Locking the front door of the house gave him good time to make his escape. Why was this so?

3 Did the murder of the Earl of Moray get the results that were desired by the Hamiltons?

4 Why do you think Elizabeth sent help to the Regent Morton quickly after the Massacre of St. Bartholemew's Eve?

5 Why do you think old women confessed to crimes of witchcraft of which they could not possibly have been guilty?

6 Why do you suppose the Lowland Scot had such a fear of the Highlanders?

7 Beds in the burgesses houses had curtains to close around them. Why was this necessary?

8 Why do you think it was thought necessary to have better educated congregations in the Church under the new system?

9 The new churches that were being built were not as grand as the old ones. Can you think of reasons why this was so?

10 The men who worked in the coal mines were bound to them like slaves. Why do you suppose this was the case?

11 Can you tell from the exports on page 70 whether or not Scotland was producing enough food for its own needs?

12 Why do you think Scotland was begining to make progress during the reign of James VI?

Further Work

1 Imagine you were one of the people in the main street of Linlithgow on 23rd January 1570. The Lord James Stewart, Earl of Moray, was making his way through the crowded street when you saw a gun barrel appear at a first floor window. You realise what was going to happen and tried to do something about it. Write the story of your unsuccessful efforts to save the 'Good Regent'.

2 The night raid on Stirling by Mary's men in 1571 would make a good picture, showing the dark horsemen against the night sky. Here is how to make such a picture.

A First make a 'model' horse by cutting out the various parts like this.

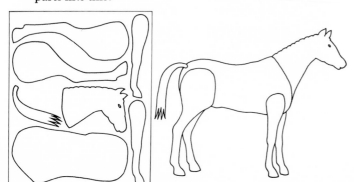

Now practise making up different galloping or trotting or standing positions of your model and then drawing the positions on another sheet of paper.

B Take a background sheet of paper and paint a night sky of cool grey-blue shades. When dry, paint a ground line in black.

C Add in very dark grey a group of horses using your model to help you. The riders should carry weapons and wear cloaks.

3 Here is what James VI had to say about a habit which we now know to be extremely dangerous. See if you know what he is talking about –

'A custom loathsome to the eye, hateful to the nose, harmful to the brain, dangerous to the lungs, and in the black stinking fume thereof, nearest resembling the horrible Stigion smoke of the pit that is bottomless'

James also wrote poetry. You will find one of his poems in the *Oxford Book of Scottish Verse*, p. 254. It is a great reprimand to another and better poet called Alexander Montgomerie. It begins.

Give patient ear to something I may say,
Beloved Sanders master of our art.
The mouse did help the lion on a day;
So I protest ye take it in good part, . . .

See if you can find this poem and others from the same period to read and enjoy.

4 Find out what you can about the imports and exports of Scotland to-day and compare these with the items and places named on page 70.

5 Old Annie had always been an outsider living as she did in the very last house in the village. Now that her husband had died leaving her destitute she had to beg. Annie found that very difficult and it made her bad temper worse. She should never have asked that old skinflint MacNab for anything – far less money. There was hardly a word exchanged before the two of them were at it hammer and tongs. Annie gave as good as she got – too good. She cursed him up and down the street. She cursed him black and she cursed him blue. The very next day MacNab's horse went lame and within the week two of his cattle had died. Then the tongues began to wag. It was Old Annie's doing, they were saying.

That little story gives you an idea how some perfectly ordinary if rather unpopular old woman comes to be accused of witchcraft. Make up a group play to perform to your class in which this kind of thing takes place.

The King and the Covenant

A parting

It was a fond if rather too hasty farewell James VI bade his subjects at St Giles on Sunday 3rd April, 1603. On the Tuesday he began slowly southward to his new throne in London promising his continued love and promising to return often, at least every three years. In England he promised his new Parliament that there would now be a united Britain, at peace and in friendship. If he was to be the kingdom's Christian head, he declared, then he could have only one body. As husband to the kingdom he could not have two wives. (Scotland and England separate.) His first promise pleased the Scots, softening the edge of their sorrow at his leaving. The second did not please the English, who had little taste for union. Swallowing Scotland had long been their ambition.

But James kept neither promise completely. He did style himself King of Great Britain, giving to all who were born after his coming to the English throne, a kind of citizenship of both realms. He did remove, for a long time, the customs paid on goods imported and exported between the countries. But the parliaments were not yet made one. He did return to Scotland, but only once and that was to be fourteen years later.

England

James liked England. He liked the fact that, for a century or more, no monarch there had been deposed, attacked, kidnapped or had died a violent death. He liked the wealth. When he had married Anne, James had borrowed a carriage and even some clothing. Now, every month, he could afford a rich new cloak and three expensive suits, six pairs of boots, and thirty pairs of gloves all in the finest hide. Now the Earl of Salisbury could lavish more than a thousand pounds (then) of hospitality and entertainment on the King during a brief five day visit. And he liked the importance of being King of England. Foreign princes paid more attention to him now.

The Church of England

But most of all James liked the support, comfort and style of the Church of England. Here there were no wild churchmen to tell him that he was only 'God's sillie vassal'* in Christ's kingdom, 'not a king nor a lord, nor a head, but a member' like everyone else. Here there were finely robed bishops to flatter him. Here he could be the true head of the Church, appointed by God to rule the souls as well as the bodies of his people.

James was quite content to govern his old northern kingdom from a comfortable desk in the south, through his council of loyal men in Scotland. But he was not content that there should be two kinds of Church in his new united kingdom. He wanted Scotland to come into line with England. And this could only mean trouble. The English Church was run by bishops – an Episcopal Church, while the Church of Scotland was Presbyterian, run by Kirk Session of ministers and elders. The Scots did not want bishops. James grew determined they would have them.

above: Portrait of James VI of Scotland, and I of England and Britain

opposite: The wealthy court of James I of England

Andrew Melville

Moves against the Scottish Church

First he prevented the General Assembly meeting and when nineteen ministers met in Aberdeen in 1605 they were summoned to appear before James's Council. They refused and were exiled for treason.

The brilliant Andrew Melville, who had greatly improved Glasgow University, and who had been the man to call James 'God's sillie vassal' was leader of the Church in Scotland. He and others were summoned to James in London, there to be taught why an Episcopal Church was better. Instead, Melville lectured the Archbishop of Canterbury on the superiority of the Presbyterian church. He even wrote a play in Latin, making fun of the kind of services he saw in James's chapel royal. For this he was sent to the Tower and then exiled in France. It suited James to be rid of Andrew Melville (who became a professor in a Huguenot University). The King could now more easily have his way.

In 1610 the bishops came to the Church of Scotland. They had been accepted by the General Assembly, packed with James's supporters. But it was still a Presbyterian church. The bishops had been tacked on. They did not replace the General Assembly nor the Kirk Sessions. They did not greatly upset the people of Scotland.

But James went further. In the summer of 1617 he made his promised and very late visit to the north. There was celebration and excitement throughout the land. It turned sour soon enough when the real reason for his three month tour became obvious. James now wanted to alter the way of worship in the Scottish Church. He tried hard to get the General Assembly to accept five changes: that there should be, where necessary, baptism at home; that Christmas, Good Friday, Easter, Ascension and Whit Sunday should all be observed as Holy Days; that children when eight should be brought to the bishop for confirmation; that Holy Communion could be given privately to the aged and sick; and that the bread and wine of Holy Communion should be taken while kneeling. Three of these changes: private communion, private baptism and keeping the Holy Days were eventually accepted by the Church of Scotland but none was acceptable then. The Assembly turned down their King's demand. James was furious and grew more determined than ever. By bribe and threat, and within the year, all five changes were forced through another General Assembly, this time at Perth. They came to be known as the Five Articles of Perth.

Now James had upset his people and they stubbornly refused to obey the new rules. Many stayed away from Church on Christmas Day; almost all were shocked to be told they must kneel as before idols to the bread and wine; even the ministers were ready to risk the King's anger by encouraging their defiant flocks. James had made a mistake and, in his last years, he came to know it. He made little effort then to enforce the Five Articles. But the damage was done.

Title page of Melville's 'Ad Scotiae'

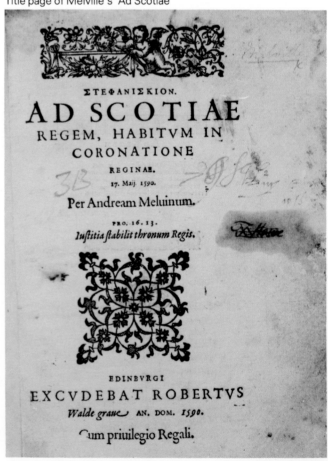

The Bible

But James had done better than this, out of his learning and honest interest in religion. He had authorised a matchless version of the Holy Bible, rich in language and style, a dignified and wonderful book that was to be the standard Word used in churches throughout his united kingdom for centuries to come. Perhaps James' Five Articles of Perth should have been a small enough price to pay for such a book.

Title page of James's Bible, 1611

Successes

And he had done better in government too. The law was better observed under James VI than ever before. Now there were courts meeting twice a year in every county. Now there were Justices of the Peace appointed to try all cases which did not deserve the death penalty. And though the Highlands remained untamed, almost a separate realm, torn with private feuds and raids, the wild borders were quieter now. Under James, Scotland had enjoyed peace and some prosperity. There had even been attempts to colonise a vast district of Canada.

James's way of ruling Scotland was a very personal one. He managed to get things done because he could manage the hearts and minds of men. He earned their friendships or their trust. In England he was not so successful because he was mistrusted by his nobles. James's claim to be the God-appointed ruler in all things of body and soul made him too powerful for their liking. He enjoyed his reign as James I of Great Britain, but it was as James VI he did his best work in government.

James died on Sunday 27th March 1625, at the home of Robert Cecil, Earl of Salisbury. He had been King of Scotland for all but the first year of his life, and of Britain for almost twenty-two years.

In 1622 Sir William Alexander, Earl of Stirling took ships and men across the North Atlantic to a bleaker, harsher place than their own, a great four hundred mile slab of land jutting into the ocean and with its north-eastern quarter broken off to be an island. It was to be the new Scotland this rolling, river-veined land of deep winter snow and heavy summer rains, of autumn fogs and late springs. But, perhaps for the want of real wealth in Scotland, Nova Scotia was never properly colonised and became little more than a name on the map. Most Scots who ventured abroad went either to settle in Ireland, or as soldiers to fight in other nations' wars. More than 50,000 found new homes in Ulster and perhaps as many as 30,000 did military service in Sweden, 6,000 in Denmark, 11,000 in France. Other Scots brigades fought in the Netherlands and Germany, in Poland and Russia. A tenth or more of the nation, now growing too fast for its food and wealth supply, left their native soil to find a new life in another land or to die there by the sword or the musket shot.

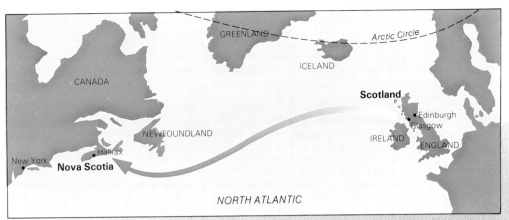

above: Gold enamelled badge of Baronet of Nova Scotia (baronetcies were awarded as incentives to settlers)

right: Cape Breton Island, Nova Scotia, as it appears today

Charles I

His son Charles now came to the throne, strong in his father's belief that kings were appointed by God. In other ways he was most unlike James. He neither understood nor cared to understand the needs of his native Scotland and it cost him dearly.

Within months of his coming to the throne the trouble began. Even then Charles I could not have guessed what lay ahead. His road was paved with good intentions. To solve some of the financial problems of Church and Crown, the King ordered, by Act of Parliament, that all the grants of Church lands and the wealth that came from them were to be withdrawn. It was Charles's good intention to make sure that money was properly shared by Crown and Church. But these rich grants had been held by nobles and landowners since Mary came to the throne more than eighty years before. After years of talk a settlement was agreed, but Charles had managed to earn the mistrust and suspicion of his Scottish nobles. The King had done the right thing in the wrong way. And he would do so again.

At last, after eight years on the throne in London, Charles came north to be crowned King of Scotland. Edinburgh had made ready. The streets were swept clean and the gruesome remains of harsh justice were removed from the city gates. The coronation took place in the Abbey Church of Holyrood amid a splendour which recalled to Scottish minds a Catholic service. At Holyrood, and in St Giles the following Sunday, there was a table like the high altar with holy books and tall candles. The English priests wore sparkling white gowns and spoke an English service.

And there was little comfort to be found in the Parliament Charles called during his visit. There, laws were passed confirming James's plan for the Scottish Church. Now there would be English services in all churches. Bishops would wear white robes, while other ministers would wear white surplices. Within three years a book of rules was published by Charles confirming the Five Articles of Perth and laying down the way in which the churches should be furnished. The communion table would be an altar and ministers would hear confession. A Scottish prayer book was being composed without the advice of Scottish ministers. Anyone opposing the new rules or criticising the leaders of Charles's Church would be excommunicated. The General Assembly and Kirk Sessions were not even mentioned.

The King's good intention was to give Scotland a better Church, more dignified and more beautiful. *The Book of Common Prayer* appeared in 1637 and with it came James VI's wonderful bible. Much that was new was good but Charles had insisted that the prayer book's first page should bear a royal command requiring its use. The beautiful volume looked too Catholic to Presbyterian eyes and they disliked commands about religion.

Portrait of Charles I

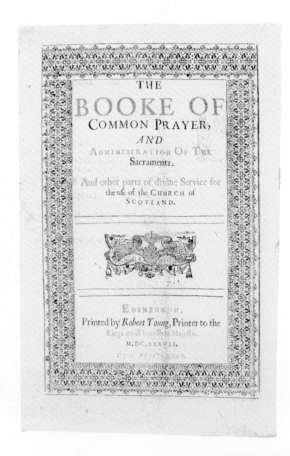

Riots in St Giles

It was on Sunday 23rd July, 1637, that Dean John Hanna rose to read the service from the new prayer book to a crowded High Church of St Giles. There before the Archbishops of Glasgow and St Andrews, the Lords of the Council, the Edinburgh Town Council, and a packed congregation, the Dean read the simple Christian prayer:

> 'Lord of all power and might, Who art the Author and Giver of all good things; Graft in our hearts the love of Thy Name, increase in us true religion, nourish us with all goodness, and of Thy great mercy keep us in the same; through Jesus Christ our Lord, Amen.'

The church exploded in ugly uproar. A stool was thrown by a woman which struck John Hanna on the head. When the Bishop of Edinburgh tried to calm the shrieking women he was greeted with cries and catcalls that he was a wolf, a witch, and that he should be hanged. The church became a deafening riot of harsh voices and shaking fists, of flying bibles, and stools wildly hurled at those who favoured the new *Book of Common Prayer*. Order was soon restored in St Giles, but the nation was now ablaze.

Charles still thinking he was right, simply ordered that the rioters were to be punished, and that his new book was to be used as he had commanded. He then went off on holiday quite unaware that the fury of the Scots was now out of control. Edinburgh was packed with angry churchfolk and ministers, burgesses and nobles. The Scots had not been so united since the days of William Wallace, Andrew Murray, Robert Bruce and the great fight for freedom. Now even the nobles joined with the people and the Capital thronged with angry demonstrators. The riot in St Giles had become a revolution.

The Covenant

By the end of February 1638, people were flocking to Kirkyard of the new Greyfriars, the first church built in Edinburgh since the Reformation. There they added their names to an agreement which bound them all in opposition to the King's new plans for the Church; those who objected to any bishops with those who would accept them along with the General Assembly and Kirk Sessions; those who denied the Five Articles of Perth with those who refused only the new Prayer Book. Together they pledged their opposition to the Catholic Church of Rome, their support of the new Protestant Faith, and their loyalty to 'our dread Sovereign, the King's Majesty, his Person and Authority.' This was the National Covenant of Scotland and like the Declaration of Arbroath it was a trumpet call to rebellion.

Worksection

The King and the Covenant
Understand your work

A Parting

1 Was James VI impatient to take up his new role as King of England as well as Scotland?
2 How did he think the two countries should be governed?
3 Did he intend to return to visit Scotland?
4 What did he do to make the two kingdoms one?
5 How did England feel about his ideas?
6 Did he keep his promise about visiting Scotland?
7 What did he like about being King of England?
8 How much was spent by the Earl of Salisbury on the King's five day stay?

The Church

1 What did James think of the Church in England?
2 What did he feel should happen to the Church of Scotland?
3 What was the main difference between these two Protestant churches?
4 How did Andrew Melville behave when James brought him to London to be taught about the Church of England?
5 What did James do about this?
6 Why did James's bishop not upset the Scots very much?
7 Why did the celebrations for James's Scottish visit in 1617 soon turn sour?
8 What were the Five Articles of Perth?
9 How did the Scottish people feel about these new Church Laws?

Successes

1 How did James improve law and order?
2 Where did the Scots try to colonise in 1622?
3 What other places did Scots go abroad to?
4 What fraction of the nation left their native land to settle elsewhere?
5 Why was James not as successful in England as he was in Scotland?
6 What was it that the English nobles objected to in James as a King?
7 How long was he King of Great Britain?

Charles I

1 What belief did Charles share with his father?
2 In what way was his attitude different?
3 How did Charles I come to be mistrusted by the Scottish nobles?
4 What was it about the coronation in the Abbey Church of Holyrood that upset the Scottish people?
5 In what ways did Charles go on upsetting the Scots?
6 Why did he do these things?
7 What was it about Dean John Hanna's simple prayer that caused a riot in the High Church of St. Giles?
8 What did the King do about the rioting?

The Covenant

1 What was the first church built in Edinburgh since the reformation?
2 What happened in the Kirkyard on February 1638?
3 What was the name of the document they were signing?
4 Did all those who signed it have exactly the same ideas?
5 Were they against the King?
6 What would be the outcome of such an agreement?

Use Your Imagination

1 Why do you think James VI did not keep his promise of regular visits to Scotland?

2 What was it that the English did not like about James's intention to govern his kingdom as one?

3 How do you think James could have made sure his kingdom was treated as one?

4 Do you think James's behaviour was affected by vanity?

5 What do you suppose it was about the Church of Scotland which upset and irritated James?

6 Was there a better way, do you think, in which James could have altered the Church of Scotland?

7 What was the most important thing in your opinion that James did for Scotland during his reign, which allowed the country to prosper?

8 How was it that James managed to get his own way in Scotland most of the time, do you think?

9 Why do you suppose large numbers of Scots went abroad to live? Do you think this is true to-day?

10 Was it Charles's intention to upset his Scottish nobles, when he made new arrangements for the lands granted to the Church and the wealth that came from them? Where do you think he went wrong?

11 He seemed to go wrong again when eventually he came north for his Scottish coronation and Parliament. How might he have arranged this differently in your opinion and perhaps pleased his subjects?

12 Charles I kept on ordering and commanding his people to do what he believed was good for them without stopping to consider what they felt or thought. Do you think this was wise, even for a King? What might he have done instead?

13 Why do you suppose King Charles did not do things differently, perhaps in the ways you have suggested?

14 What had he managed to do with his people in Scotland instead of getting them to unite in one Church, like the Church of England?

15 Even though the Scots were opposed to what Charles was doing the National Covenant of Scotland pledged loyalty to 'our dread Sovereign, the King's Majesty, his Person and Authority'? Why do you suppose this was so?

Further Work

1 A year or two after James had become King of England there was a plot against his life and against the Westminster Parliament. It was called the Gunpowder Plot, and it is still remembered on the 5th November each year. Find out all you can about Guido Fawkes and the other conspirators.

2 It was James who authorised the version of the Holy Bible still in general use to-day. The very first page of every copy carries the dedication from the translaters to King James. You may find it interesting to read this, and to see how our language has changed from the time of King James.

3 In October 1949 the Scottish National Party launched a new National Covenant which again pledged loyalty to the Crown but this time was demanding a Scottish Parliament with proper powers. Almost two million people signed it. You can find the text of this new covenant in a book called '*The Flag in the Wind*', by J MacCormick (p. 128). You may find it interesting to read.

4 In a radio play sound effects are used to make places and actions seem real. Make a list of all the sounds your group can think of that you would hear on Sir William Alexander's ships, like whistling wind, flapping sails, creaking boards, rubbing ropes, shouted orders, lapping water, dripping rain, calling sea birds, footsteps on deck, thunder, and so on.

   Now, work out ways of making these sound effects – blowing on the edge of paper, rubbing hands together, creaking an old chair or door etc. When you have done this you could either record them for use in the play below, or prepare them to be performed by the whole class as a band or orchestra. You would have to arrange who was to play what, when!

5 On the long voyages of discovery there were always risks of mutiny as sailors became alarmed about their safety. Here is the beginning of such a play about a possible mutiny. See if your group can carry on the play and decide whether the mutiny takes place or not.

The Mutiny

Thomas: Shut the hatch, and let's talk.

Rob: (NERVOUSLY) I don't know if we should, you know. Anyway, what about?

Jock: You know well enough, lily liver! About this stinking rat-trap of a ship, about wormy biscuits and filthy water, about this crack-brained voyage; about that lunatic so-called Admiral on the poop . . .

Rob: For goodness sake, not so loud! You'll have us all hanging from a yard-arm!

Jock: Coward!

Thomas: That's enough Jock. He may be a coward, but he's got a lot more sense than you.

Joe: And a better sense of God's will, Jock. That evil temper of yours will lead you to the devil, for sure.

Thomas: Spare us the sermon, holy one, and turn your clever mind to this. And the rest of you, too. Are we for turning back now? And if we are, how are we going to do it? And if we do it how are we going to get away with it?

Rob: Sssh! Somebody's coming!

Rebellion

A loyalist revolt

The Covenanters called their own General Assembly in November 1638 at Glasgow, with the King's unwilling approval. There they abolished bishops, books of prayer and the Five Articles of Perth. Charles angrily declared the Assembly and its actions unlawful. Yet the Covenanters had a sworn loyalty to their King and when they appointed the next General Assembly to meet the following summer they added 'unless his Majesty should otherwise appoint.'

But Charles did not think them loyal. They were rebels to be put down by force. He summoned his army and made ready for war. North of the border the Scots prepared too.

Behind Alexander Leslie and beneath a blue banner bearing the words 'For Christ's Crown and Covenant' they marched, twenty thousand strong. They made camp on the gentle rise of Dunse Law, twelve miles west of Berwick where the King's men stood. The Covenanters, force was strong and well prepared, its ranks swelled by battle-hardened troops recalled from service in Sweden. But as they sang their psalms and listened to the pipes and fiddles they were troubled by the memory of oaths of loyalty to the King they were preparing to fight. The King's army was ill-prepared and hungry, unwilling to face a strong enemy. There was no battle. Instead Charles gave the Covenanters promises which he did not mean to keep and which they did not believe he would. The armies would meet again.

By August the following year the King had broken his word and the Scottish army was marching south once more. This time it was led by James Graham, Earl of Montrose, and this time it crossed the border. Montrose showed his men that it was safe to wade the River Tweed by doing so himself – three times in full kit. They met the King's force where it bravely barred the crossing at Newburn Ford on the River Tyne. The Covenanters guns blew the defenders aside and the great host surged across the river and on to Newcastle on the 30th August, 1640. This time the Scots would make no bargains with their King alone. This time they would speak to the English Parliament. A treaty was finally agreed in June 1641 by which the King gave bitter approval to all the General Assembly had decided. And more than that, the Scots were paid £300,000 in expenses by the Northern Counties. Not only was it a total bloodless victory for the Covenanters, but the English had been made to pay for the privilege of being occupied by a Scottish army. But it was not the end of the war.

Alexander Leslie and the Covenanters on the march

Charles and Parliament

Charles was now in the throes of a bitter power struggle with his English Parliament. His firm belief that he was God-appointed ruler of all and right in everything was a stumbling block to all reasonable negotiations. He always gave way too late to his subjects' reasonable wishes, by which time they had become less reasonable. In the end he granted almost all they asked for but none of it soon enough or sincerely enough.

Perhaps Charles delayed because he felt sure his opponents would, sooner or later, fight amongst themselves. Already things were less happy in the victorious Scotland than they should have been. Already the Covenanters were disagreeing amongst themselves. Montrose and others were now troubled by the growing power of the Earl of Argyll. There was even talk of deposing the King and yet the Covenant demanded loyalty. And Montrose disliked too the change in the mood of the Covenanters. Now people were *compelled* to sign the Covenant, which itself spoke of liberty.

It was in this atmosphere of distrust and with Montrose already imprisoned for his over-loyalty to Charles, that the King made a desperate visit to Edinburgh late in the summer of 1641. He hoped to find allies against the English Parliament. Royal flattery and royal honours won him no support save a few frail promises. Montrose who could have advised him was not released from prison until after his departure.

Soon after his return to London, Charles burst into the House of Commons to try and arrest five of its most troublesome members. They all escaped. The storm broke and on the 22nd August 1642, Charles raised his Royal Standard at Nottingham. England was at war with itself and both sides looked to Scotland for help. For aid to the King, the Covenanters demanded no less than a Scottish-style Church in England. For aid to Parliament they asked the same. But Parliament, losing the war, was prepared to offer most in return for aid from Scotland.

The Civil War in England

In the winter frost of 1644, Alexander Leslie, now Earl of Leven, led a Scots army of more than twenty thousand foot and horse across the frozen Tweed and south into England, driving the English royalist forces before them. He had been made an Earl by Charles for promising not to do this! A few miles west of York on Marston Moor the Scots joined forces with Oliver Cromwell's Parliament troops. They faced Prince Rupert of the Rhine, the brilliant and victorious leader of the King's men. On the 2nd July, the harder of the Scots pikemen set themselves in stubborn schiltron against the lancing charges of Rupert's cavalry. With Cromwell injured and his own soldiers in confusion, David Leslie led eight hundred mounted Scots against the triumphant Royal cavalry and brought them to a halt in a defiant fury of slashing blades. Their squadrons broken, Rupert's men fled the field. Parliament had won its first victory. Charles had lost his cause. But the Scots got little enough credit and little payment for the part they played at Marston Moor. They withdrew to Newcastle hurt and angry.

The Battle of Marston Moor

Montrose

North of the border James Graham, Earl of Montrose, had been wrestling with his own conscience. He was a loyal Covenanter, amongst the very first to have signed the great National Covenant. But so much was now changed. It seemed to him that the King had granted what the Covenant required. What was now being asked went far beyond its terms, even against its spirit. He could not support the English Parliament against the King. He could not remain faithful to the National Covenant and be loyal to those who had changed its purpose.

In the end Montrose made his way to Oxford, and offered his services to an ungrateful and undeserving monarch. He was eventually accepted by Charles and appointed lieutenant-general of the King's forces in Scotland – but given no forces. His mind cleared of doubt Montrose now declared that he was fighting on the King's side for the same reasons that he had fought for the Covenant. He was still defending and keeping 'the true Protestant religion, his Majesty's just and sacred authority, the fundamental laws and privileges of Parliament, the peace and freedom of the oppressed and enthralled subject.' It was because he believed Charles I stood for these things, and only for as long as he believed this, that Montrose had taken up arms in the royal cause. It was what the National Covenant had proclaimed when it proudly bound Covenanters to 'defend the true religion and recover the purity and liberty of the gospel' and to 'stand to the defence of our dread sovereign, the King's Majesty, his Person and Authority; in the defence and preservation of the foresaid true religion, liberties, and laws of the Kingdom.'

It was March 1644 when James Graham, Earl of Montrose, rode north out of Oxford. When he met with Prince Rupert at a Richmond inn only two days after Marston Moor he was refused the thousand horse he needed to carry the King's cause into Scotland. Instead Montrose handed over his own small troop and entered Scotland with two friends dressed as Leven's soldiers. Montrose followed as their groom.

They plodded north on their desperate journey through the Lowlands where Covenant patrols kept watch. They were hardly across the border and clear of Netherby woods when a Scots trooper joined their company and for all their disguise immediately addressed Montrose by his title. Denials were useless and brushed aside by the man as he exclaimed, 'What, do I not know my Lord Marquis of Montrose well enough? But go your way and God be with you.' They breathed again and pushed forward more carefully and more tensely than before.

At last and with great relief, the riders reached the safety of a friendly Tower House at Tullybelton.

From there Montrose raised a modest force of Highland clansmen who had more quarrel with the Earl of Argyll and his Campbells than with the King, about whom they knew or cared little enough. Now Montrose waited to meet with the sixteen hundred MacDonalds and MacLeans from Ireland, led by the giant Alasdair MacDonald, sometimes called Alasdair Mac-Coll Chiotach after his father who had been nicknamed Coll Chiotach – Coll the left-handed. In the Lowlands the name became Colkitto and would not be forgotten.

A first blow

On the rising ground of Glen Tilt, Montrose called his men to the Royal Standard, not much over two and a half thousand of them and not well armed. Three horses were his only cavalry and the muskets the Highlanders carried had but one bullet each. They depended more on the power of the bow and the thrust of pike and claymore, club and dagger. But they were Highlanders in their Highlands, hunters by nature and long practice. They would yet be a dangerous foe for lowland farmers. But first they needed supplies and for these they would have to fight.

It was on the second to last day of August 1644 that Montrose and his ragged band swung out of Blair Athol and along Loch Tummel's northern edge. They turned south by high peaked Schiehallion's great eastern spread towards Aberfeldy and across the shining Tay. They were quick. Having brushed aside a challenge at Castle Menzies, they were drawn up on Sunday 1st September to face a very confident army of the Covenant which barred their way three miles west of Perth at Tibbermore. Seven thousand strong, these Covenanters had been promised an easy victory by over-excited ministers, and saw no reason to doubt it in the thin straggle of men that faced them, outnumbered almost three to one.

With a battle cry of 'Jesus and no quarter', which seems a strange idea, they advanced to put an end to the Irish Catholics and wild Highlanders. Montrose's reply was a spattering volley of precious bullets and a hail of stones. It scattered the over-confident cavalry. The screaming Highland charge of Colkitto's Irish chilled the hearts of the ministers' men and the battle was a rout. Perth had fallen and Montrose had found supplies. Now it was north to Aberdeen.

Montrose was pressed for time. Argyll was closing with a powerful force. Victory had to be swift, but it came only after a dour struggle. A dangerous charge by the horsemen of Sir William Forbes of Craigievar would have been more serious had it not been against Colkitto's men. As the horses thundered on to them they opened their ranks and let them pass through, turning as they did to empty the saddles with musket fire. The charge turned quickly to flight. Another charge, this time by the Irish, shocked the defenders into sudden defeat. The city was won and there followed three black days when defenceless citizens who might have favoured Montrose were put to the sword in a frenzy of looting and murder. In that single act of rash brutality Montrose lost much. When he entered the city and saw for himself the horrors of

what he had permitted, he brought it to an end. For the rest of his campaign he would hold his men on the tightest rein. No further outrage would be committed in his name. But the damage was done and he would get no support in the Lowlands.

Montrose left Aberdeen only three days before Argyll, whose mighty army came grimly in pursuit of the Montrose and King's men. Through glowing autumn and into white mountain winter the merry dance went on from glen to glen.

As he had done at Perth, Montrose sent forward a demand for surrender by a messenger with a drummer boy. They were well received by the magistrates who gave the lad a silver coin. As the

two returned under the flag of truce the young drummer boy, by mistake or intent, was shot dead. In his rage Montrose promised Aberdeen to Colkitto's men, to do with it as they pleased.

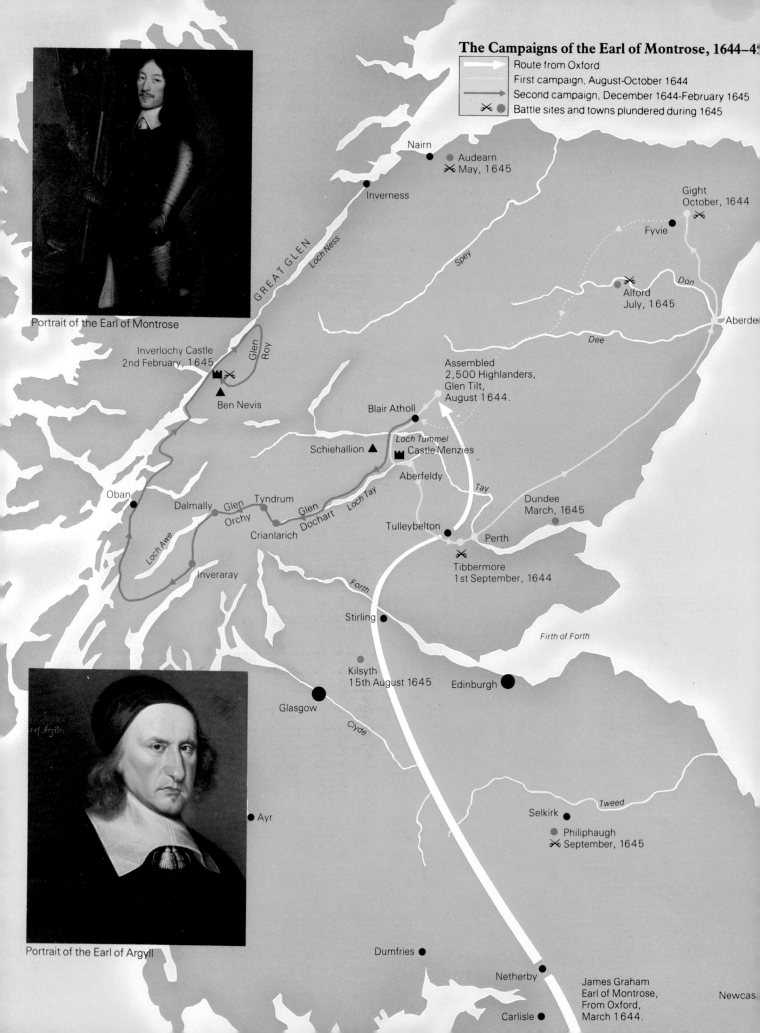

The Campaigns of the Earl of Montrose, 1644–45

Route from Oxford
First campaign, August-October 1644
Second campaign, December 1644-February 1645
Battle sites and towns plundered during 1645

Nairn

Audearn
May, 1645

Inverness

Gight
October, 1644

Fyvie

GREAT GLEN

Loch Ness

Spey

Alford
July, 1645

Don

Aberde

Inverlochy Castle
2nd February, 1645

Glen Roy

Ben Nevis

Dee

Assembled
2,500 Highlanders,
Glen Tilt,
August 1644.

Blair Atholl

Schiehallion

Loch Tummel
Castle Menzies

Oban

Aberfeldy

Tay

Dundee
March, 1645

Dalmally   Glen   Tyndrum

Orchy   Glen   Loch Tay

Loch Awe   Crianlarich   Dochart

Tulleybelton

Perth

Tibbermore
1st September, 1644

Inveraray

Forth

Stirling

Firth of Forth

Kilsyth
15th August 1645

Edinburgh

Glasgow

Clyde

Ayr

Tweed

Selkirk

Philiphaugh
September, 1645

Portrait of the Earl of Montrose

Portrait of the Earl of Argyll

Dumfries

Netherby

James Graham
Earl of Montrose,
From Oxford,
March 1644.

Newcas

Carlisle

Montrose caught

In late October, while Colkitto's force was away on private raiding, the Earl of Argyll came close enough to grasp the heels of his nimble quarry. The four thousand foot and horse of the Covenanters eagerly chased the King's men into the rising ground of Gight, a mile or two east of Fyvie in Aberdeenshire. There they closed for the kill. From their hillside ditches the men of Montrose struck back and struck hard. Hard enough to seize muskets on their first attack and the ammunition on a second. Argyll crossed the River Ythan to nurse his wounded pride, before withdrawing to Inverary, the capital of the Clan Campbell country. Montrose vanished.

That December, by drove road and pack trail, through sleet swept passes and over high white mountain shoulders, Montrose led his ragged band once more from Blair down between Tummel and Loch Rannoch and past Schiehallion. But this time they swept westward by the long shores of Loch Tay. With Colkitto now returned they were three thousand strong, each a clansman nursing some private anger at past hurts from Campbell hands.

A surprise attack

By now Argyll knew that Montrose was advancing but believed that no army could cross the winter hills. He settled to improving the defences of his castle and making plans for spring. Yet on through Glen Dochart, and down wild Glen Orchy, Montrose was coming, by Crianlarich and Tyndrum to Dalmally at the head waters of Loch Awe. Only then, with the din of Colkitto's pipes ringing in their ears did Argyll's frantic men raise the alarm and rush the news to Inverary that the King's Lieutenant was upon them. Argyll escaped by herring boat leaving his lands and his people to the revenge of the invaders. They plundered and burned until January, but there was no slaughter.

Though he had no news yet of Argyll, Montrose marched north out of the Campbell lands in the middle of January. He knew that soon enough the great clan would muster to settle the score. Ahead lay the winter highlands and five thousand Mackenzies raised against him. To the east was the Covenanting army and to the west only the grey Atlantic. Now he learned that Argyll and three thousand Campbells were at his heels. Montrose was trapped in the Great Glen and the most savage of winter weather was now closing in. Through blizzard and snowdrift, with little food and no rest, Montrose wheeled fifteen hundred men, south again, but not down the Great Glen where the Campbells were. Instead in the early hours of

Friday 31st January, 1645, he led his men into the teeth of the winter gales, up and over the snow clad mountain barrier which no one believed could be crossed. Through narrow ravines they threaded their swift passage, down through Glen Roy and over the mighty shoulder of Ben Nevis. Beneath them suddenly was Inverlochy Castle in whose shadow Clan Campbell rested. By dusk on that February evening Montrose's weary column had gathered unseen for what rest and refreshment they might find in that stark, bleak winter place.

At first light on 2nd February, Argyll's senses were shocked by the blast of royal war horns. He knew that by some desperate miracle Montrose was come. The dawn broke to the fierce skirl of Colkitto's pipes. Battle was joined. Once again Argyll escaped by ship from the rout and slaughter that followed. The Campbells were crushed, and by a tired outnumbered force. It seemed that Montrose could never be beaten.

But his army had to eat and be supplied. Risk was the price to be paid. While the victors plundered Dundee, under Montrose's watchful eye, it was learned that a powerful Covenanting army was less than a mile away. Panic seized all but the King's Lieutenant. With the same power of command that had brought together the Highland clans and Colkitto's Irish at Blair the previous summer, Montrose now pulled his half-drunk men from their plunder. He led them to safety through the East Port of Dundee as the Covenanters entered the West Port. It was another of Montrose's desperate miracles.

And he won more battles, always outnumbered, never out-thought – at Auldearn by Nairn on the Moray Firth in May, and at Alford twenty or so miles east of Aberdeen on the Don in July. But in June Charles had been crushingly defeated at Naseby, south of Market Harborough in Northampton. It was time for Montrose to come out of the highlands to the aid of his King.

At Kilsyth, thirteen miles north-east of Glasgow, on the 15th August, the King's Lieutenant faced the Covenanting forces once more. In the warm calm of high summer he drove six thousand of the Ministers' men from the field and few escaped with their lives.

Coat of arms of the Earl of Argyll

Victory

Montrose now commanded all Scotland. He had won back the kingdom for his King and he felt able to summon a parliament to meet in Glasgow on the 20th October. But his faithful Highlanders, who had always preferred to fight for plunder and revenge rather than Covenants and Kings, began to melt away. They were disappointed not to have the looting of Glasgow, the fattest and juiciest prize of a whole year's fighting. They felt the need to look to the defence of their glens.

With only six hundred men and Colkitto gone to bother the Campbells again, Montrose pushed south to find a new army and march to the rescue of his King in honour of his pledge. He got no further than Selkirk. There through the autumn mist that hung low over the meadowland by Ettrick Water came the onrush of Covenanting horse led by Leslie. Outnum-

bered ten to one, the King's men fought with stubborn courage, attacking like demons the huge force arrayed against them. In the end, and only after a mighty struggle, they were overpowered. Montrose would have fought to the death had he not been taken from the field by friends. The few men who survived the battle and surrendered on the promise of mercy, got none. The ministers now demanded in the name of God the slaughter of the defeated soldiers, three hundred women and children, and two hundred or so cooks, horse boys and the like. Even Leslie's hardened soldiers sickened of their work before the ministers were sated.

And so ended Montrose's golden year of triumph. There would be no other. In the following May, Charles I surrendered himself to a Covenanting army in England and ordered Montrose to disband his army and leave the country.

The Battle of Selkirk

The King prisoner

Since their great victory at Marston Moor, the Scots army was unhappy and unused in England. Now they held Charles I and were anxious to return home. But neither would the King accept the Covenant nor would the English Parliament pay the promised expenses to the Scots. In the end they left England with only a tenth of the two million pounds they claimed. And they left without Charles who, still refusing the Covenant, was handed over to the English Parliament, on condition that he would not be harmed.

But the English army was growing stronger. Led by Oliver Cromwell, it ruled the land rather than Parliament. They seized the King in the June of 1647 and some Scottish nobles now made plans to help him. With secret promises from Charles that he would give the Presbyterian Church a three year trial in England, they raised an army and marched against Cromwell. It was a powerful enough force but badly trained and led. Much of Scotland was against the King and the campaign. Cromwell crushed these 'Engagers' as they were called at Preston in August of 1648.

The Church in command

It was the Earl of Argyll who now became master of Scotland. He made an agreement with Cromwell that none of the Engagers would be given work of importance or trust. And he went further. In January 1649, the Scottish Parliament passed the Act of Classes which prevented all kinds of people from holding public office: those who had supported Montrose's rebellion; the Engagers themselves; any who had shown sympathy with them or had not opposed them; those who did not behave properly or who missed family worship. The ministers of the church decided who might be in the last group.

Execution of the King

What peace the agreement with Cromwell might have brought to Scotland was soon shattered. On 30th January 1649, Cromwell's men executed Charles I. All Scotland was shocked. Argyll was outraged. At once he turned to the King's son, now in Holland for his own safety, and had him proclaimed King Charles II. Now there would be war.

Charles II was not too keen to come to Scotland. He believed the nation had delivered his father into the hands of his enemies. He was not at all happy about accepting the Solemn League and Covenant. Montrose, also an exile, seemed the answer. In 1650, in the spring and with only his King's good wishes and not much more than a thousand raw troops, Montrose marched again in Scotland. At Carbisdale, away to the north on the Dornoch Firth, on 27th April, he was surprised and defeated. He was betrayed for twenty five thousand pounds Scots, and handed over to the government. In Edinburgh on 21st May 1650, James Graham, Earl of Montrose and Viceroy of Scotland was hanged. Those who had come to jeer, even paid to hurl stones, were quietened by his dignity and bearing in death. To the end he was loyal to the National Covenant declaring just before his execution, 'The Covenant which I took, I own it and adhere to it. Bishops, I care not for them. I never intended to advance their interests. But when the King granted you all your desires and you were every one sitting under his vine and fig tree – that then you should have taken a party in England by the hand and entered into a league with them against the King, was the thing I judged my duty to oppose you to the yondmost.'

Cartoon of Charles II

Portrait of Charles II

Charles II

A month after that execution Charles II arrived in Scotland, ready to sign the Covenant and to be King. Cromwell, Lord Protector of England, had other ideas. He came north to ask the General Assembly to think again about Charles, to 'think it possible you may be mistaken.' But the Assembly, God appointed and right in all things, was not in the habit of thinking itself mistaken. The Lord Protector knew this. He brought with him sixteen thousand well trained men to make his plea better heard. At Dunbar on 3rd September 1650, he met a Scottish army of the Covenant led by David Leslie, but hampered by a committee of ministers who barred from the fight all who were unworthy to bear arms under the terms of the foolish Act of Classes. They also, as such committees had done before, gave a great deal of advice on the conduct of the battle. Leslie listened and Cromwell won.

Battle of Worcester

And he won again even more crushingly at Worcester exactly one year later when Charles II, now crowned King at Scone, and Leslie, led a mightier Scots host. Its ranks were not reduced this time by the ministers' committee. The Act of Classes had been abolished that June. Cromwell let them march deep in to England and then followed, waiting his chance to pounce. The struggle when it came was brief and bitter, a few hours under a late summer sun. Charles fled the country and Cromwell was master of both kingdoms. There was no government in Scotland and no monarch, only a Lord Protector who now declared Scotland and England to be but one commonwealth and subject to his single rule.

The Battle of Worcester

Worksection

Rebellion
Understand your work

A Loyalist revolt
1 What did the Covenanters do in November 1638?
2 What actions were taken at this meeting?
3 How did King Charles I feel about the Covenanters?
4 Why did no battle take place at Duns Law?
5 Did the King keep his promises?
6 Who led the Covenanters in August 1640?
7 How did James Graham, Earl of Montrose show that it was safe to wade the River Tweed?
8 What were the terms of the treaty agreed by the King in June 1641?

Charles and Parliament
1 What did Charles believe upset the negotiations he had with the English Parliament?
2 What may Charles have hoped would happen if he delayed long enough?
3 Why was Montrose unhappy about the Covenanters?
4 Why did King Charles visit Edinburgh in the summer of 1641, and was he successful?
5 Who could have advised the King about his visit and why did he not?
6 What did Charles do which finally brought on civil war?
7 What did the Scots demand as their price for aid to either side?
8 Why were Parliament prepared to pay that price?

The Civil War in England
1 Why had Alexander Leslie been made the Earl of Leven?
2 How did the Scottish troops cross the Tweed in 1644?
3 At what battle did the Scots army face the King's men?
4 Who was the leader of the Royal forces?
5 How did the Scots help to win the battle for Parliament?
6 Why did they feel hurt and angry?

Montrose
1 Why did Montrose find himself wrestling with his conscience?
2 Did the King deserve Montrose's loyalty?
3 What made his position as Lieutenant-General of the King's forces in Scotland very difficult?
4 What was Montrose fighting for?
5 Why did he decide to support the King?
6 What happened to the arrangement by which Montrose was to receive a thousand horses from Prince Rupert?
7 What happened to Montrose and his companions when they crossed the border in disguise?
8 Who was Montrose to meet with at Blair Athol?
9 What does the name Alasdair Coll Chiotach mean?
10 How was it remembered in the Lowlands?

A First Blow
1 Where did Montrose first raise the Royal Standard in Scotland?
2 How was his force made up and armed?
3 Where and when did they first face the army of the Covenant?
4 Why were the Covenanters confident of victory?
5 What decided the battle?
6 Why was Montrose in a hurry?
7 How did Colkitto's men deal with the dangerous charge of Forbes's cavalry?
8 What caused Montrose to allow Aberdeen to be sacked by Colkitto's men? Did he regret this decision?
9 What was the lasting result of this rash and angry decision?
10 By how long did Montrose escape his pursuers at Aberdeen?

Montrose caught
1 Where was Montrose caught by the Earl of Argyll?
2 Why was Montrose's army weaker than usual?
3 How did Montrose deal with Argyll's attack?
4 Where did Argyll go after his defeat?
5 What route did Montrose follow?
6 Why was Argyll not expecting Montrose to attack again?
7 Where did Montrose strike this time?
8 Where did Montrose find himself trapped?
9 How did he escape the trap and attack again?
10 Where was the battle this time?
11 Why did Montrose plunder Dundee?
12 How did he show his amazing powers of command in Dundee?
13 Where did Montrose finally defeat the Covenanters?

Victory
1 What was Montrose able to do in the October of 1645 in Glasgow?
2 What caused the faithful Highlanders to leave for their glens?
3 Why did Montrose march south with such a small army?
4 How much larger was the Covenanting Army than Montrose's at Selkirk?
5 What happened to those who surrendered to the Covenanters?
6 Who else suffered the same fate?
7 Who urged the soldiers to carry out this work?
8 By whose order were Montrose's efforts brought to an end?

The King Prisoner
1 Why had the Scots lingered in England?
2 To whom did they hand over the King and on what conditions?
3 Who tried to help King Charles when he was seized by Cromwell?
4 What did the Act of Classes do?

5 What ended hopes of a peaceful agreement between the Scots and Cromwell?

Charles II

1 Why was Charles II unwilling to come to Scotland?
2 What did he do instead?
3 When did he finally come?
4 What did Cromwell do about the decision taken by the General Assembly's proclamation that Charles II was King?
5 What hampered the Scots army at Dunbar in 1650?
6 What did Cromwell declare after he had won the Battle of Worcester?

Use Your Imagination

1 Why do you think the Scots would make no bargains with the King at Newcastle?

2 Why do you suppose Scotland was particularly pleased with the terms of the treaty agreed in 1641?

3 What was it about Charles I that caused his subjects to become stronger and less reasonable in their attitudes?

4 Who do you think the King should have consulted when he was in Edinburgh?

5 Why do you suppose Charles did not think it necessary to get help from the Scots by accepting the terms of the Solemn League and Covenant and guaranteeing a Presbyterian Church?

6 Why did Montrose think that he had to support the King?

7 Why is the battle cry – 'Jesus and no quarter' a very strange one indeed?

8 Are you surprised that Montrose allowed the Sack of Aberdeen after the killing of the young drummer boy? What do you suppose he thought about it afterwards?

9 Why do you think Montrose decided to lead his men over the winter mountains and attack Argyll at Inverary only a month or so after the narrow escape from the Covenanters near Fyvie?

10 What do you think made the Highlanders not a very relible army for long campaigns?

11 In your opinion did Charles deserve the loyalty that was shown to him? How much do you think he was to blame himself for his own downfall?

12 Some people argue that Montrose was the only man who stayed true to the National Covenant. Do you think this could be correct?

Further Work

1 There must have been many times in the Civil War when soldiers stood about in the miserable wet weather just waiting for something to happen. Here is how to make a picture of such a soldier, cold and dejected in the grey winter rain.

You will need some white cartridge paper or typing paper about A4 size, a soft pencil (2B); some grey tinted paper; paste and scissors.

The Background
Divide the white paper about a third from the bottom with ground lines and add some puddles. Draw grass blades carefully along this.

grasses

Fill in the spaces between the puddles with pebbles and stones.

The Foreground
Now take the grey tinted paper and cut out a tree for your soldier to shelter under. Carefully stick this close to one edge of your picture. Trim off any part that overlaps the edge of your picture.
Now with your pencil add a bark pattern.

The Soldier
(He should be about *half* the height of your picture)
It would help if someone poses leaning on a pole as a cold, tired soldier might do on his pike. Draw this figure on the grey paper and, when the shape is right, add the uniform and weapons. (Use an illustration to help you.)
Cut out your figure and stick in position under the tree.

The Finishing Touches
Add, with great care, the heavy steady rain in straight slanting lines over everything and making rings in the puddles.

2 There is a book by John Buchan called *Montrose* in which you will find much more about his exciting exploits. Try to get a copy and learn more about the Marquis.

3 Imagine you are with Montrose on his marshes and write of an adventure in which you play a vital part. Use your map to help you decide where and when it happened. By using the right place names and dates you can make your story seem more real.

Acknowledgements

Moffat: A History of Scotland, Book 3
The Publisher would like to thank the following for permission to reproduce photographs:

Bodleian Library, Oxford, 66 (bottom left); John Brennan, Oxford, 51, 52 (bottom left & right); Bridgeman Art Library, 36 (right); British Library, 41, 43, 47, 66 (centre & top right), 76 (bottom right), 80 (bottom right); Colorific!, 79 (right); Edinburgh University Library, 19 (bottom right); Faculty of Advocates, Edinburgh, 24 (bottom); Fotomax Index, 77, 92; H.M. the Queen Collection, 56; Robert Harding, 74; La Goélette, Paris, 31 (left), 43; Mansell Collection, 7, 38 (bottom right); National Gallery of Scotland, 57; National Library of Scotland, 22 (top), 45; National Museum of Antiquities of Scotland, 4 (left), 66 (top left), 79 (top left); National Portrait Gallery, 36 (left), 44 (right), 54, 63 (left), 65 (left), 80 (bottom left), 93 (top); Public Records Office, 38 (left); Royal Commission of Ancient and Historic Monuments of Scotland, 71; Royal Scottish Musum, 21 (right); Scottish National Portrait Gallery, 4 (right), 11 (top right), 19 (top left), 29, 32 (right), 38 (top right), 44 (left), 52 (top), 59, 63 (right), 65 (right), 88 (top & bottom); University of St Andrews, 11 (top left), 76 (top left); Victoria and Albert Museum, 37 (top); Vision International, 32 (top left), Wellcome Institute Library, London, 19 (bottom left), Worcester City Museum, 93 (bottom).

Illustrations by Victor Ambrus, Robert Ayton, Stephen Cocking, Richard Hook, Andrew Howat, John James, Tony Morris, David Palmer, Roger Payne, Peter Sarson, John Smith and Michael Whittlesea.